WORLD BANK STAFF WORKING PAPERS
Number 527

Worker-Peasant Education in the People's Republic of China

Adult Education during the Post-Revolutionary Period

Nat J. Colletta

The World Bank
Washington, D.C., U.S.A.

This is a working document published informally by The World Bank. To present the results of research with the least possible delay, the typescript has not been prepared in accordance with the procedures appropriate to formal printed texts, and The World Bank accepts no responsibility for errors. The publication is supplied at a token charge to defray part of the cost of manufacture and distribution.

The views and interpretations in this document are those of the author(s) and should not be attributed to The World Bank, to its affiliated organizations, or to any individual acting on their behalf. Any maps used have been prepared solely for the convenience of the readers; the denominations used and the boundaries shown do not imply, on the part of The World Bank and its affiliates, any judgment on the legal status of any territory or any endorsement or acceptance of such boundaries.

The full range of The World Bank publications is described in the *Catalog of World Bank Publications;* the continuing research program of the Bank is outlined in *World Bank Research Program: Abstracts of Current Studies.* Both booklets are updated annually; the most recent edition of each is available without charge from the Publications Distribution Unit of the Bank in Washington or from the European Office of the Bank, 66, avenue d'Iéna, 75116 Paris, France.

Library of Congress Cataloging in Publication Data

Colletta, Nat J.
Worker-peasant education in the Peoples Republic of China.

(World Bank staff working papers ; no. 527)
Bibliography: p.
1. Adult education and state--China--History--20th century. 2. Labor and laboring classes--Education--China--History--20th century. I. Title. II. Series.
LC5389.C6C64 1982 374'.951 82-11165
ISBN 0-8213-0050-4

ABSTRACT OF THE STUDY

This paper reviews and analyzes adult education activities in China from the late 1920s to the present time. First, it examines briefly the changing face of adult education in relation to the larger political economic transformations which have taken place in China; and second, it describes and draws lessons from the present policy, programs, and objectives of worker-peasant education in China. Methodologically, the paper draws on field observations and individual interviews conducted during a twenty-four day study mission to the PRC; on-site program briefs collected during visits to major institutions of worker-peasant education, e.g., factories, communes, mass organizations, etc.; field notes from symposiums or large group exchanges; and a review of the relevant literature on Chinese worker-peasant education. The study concludes that the most important functions of adult education have been political socialization, the solving of practical problems in industry and agriculture, and the raising of the basic educational level of the masses. The relative priority of these aspects has shifted over the past few decades with ideological shifts. Presently, the educational pendulum is swinging toward the intitutionalization of adult education programs with emphasis on quality and legitimacy (Credentialling) over equality and access. A number of major lessons emerge from the Chinese experience in adult education. First, that the mobilization of political will, the creation of a strong bureaucratic organization, and the establishment of a definitive planning process which can effectively coordinate user demands with the delivery of services are a *sine qua non* of success. A second major lesson lies in the Chinese use of "modeling", "meetings", and "on-spot conferences", among other *ad hoc* group arrangements in a decentralized but controlled system for promoting the exchange of experience and technology. A third lesson rests in the Chinese ability to mobilize unused and underutilized resources, both human and material. A fourth major lesson lies in the area of motivation or "popularization" techniques for promoting user participation and subsequent service demand creation. While success has been marked, many problems such as rural-urban inequities, the potential risk of losing the relevance of programs to local needs through an emphasis on the formalization of adult education, among others, still remain. Recommendations for more empirical evaluation of adult education programs, particularly focusing on such studies as the comparative cost-effectiveness of on-job versus vocational school training, the differential impact of various forms of mass media, among others, are given.

The author is a loan officer with the East Asia and Pacific Regional Office of the World Bank.

Table of Contents

Introduction

1. Since the 1920s, China has relied heavily on adult education to effect desired changes in political ideology, socio-economic relations, and human productive capabilities. The belief in the power of education in general, and adult education in particular, to create a "new socialist person" and construct a "new social order" has at times reached religious proportions. The cyclical shifts in ideological fervor and accompanying socio-economic development strategies have been mirrored in the relative emphasis placed on agricultural versus industrial development, quantitative versus qualitative orientations, mass versus elite education, and more specifically, nonformal versus formal school education. Even within a particular educational mode such as adult education, the focus has continually shifted between peasant and worker education (Pepper, 1978, 1980; Lofstedt, 1980; Chen, 1974, 1978; Shirk, 1979).

2. The purpose of this paper is twofold: first, to examine briefly the changing face of adult education in relation to the larger political-economic transformations which have taken place in China over the past three decades; and second, to describe and draw lessons from the present policy, programs, and objectives of worker-peasant education in the People's Republic of China (PRC) today. For the purposes of this paper the terms 'adult education' and 'worker-peasant education' differ in that adult education activities not only include worker-peasant education under the Bureau of Worker-Peasant Education, Ministry of Education, but also adult educational activities under the auspices of other line Ministries. The focus of this paper is on those activities under the Bureau.

/1 I would like to take this opportunity to thank the International Council for Adult Education (ICAE), particularly Mr. Budd Hall, Director General of ICAE and Mr. Roby Kidd, Head of the China-ICAE project; Mr. Aklilu Habte of the World Bank Education Department; Messrs. R. Stern, E.V.K. Jaycox, and C. Koch-Weser of the East Asia and Pacific Programs Department, World Bank; and Mr. Zang Boping, Vice-Minister of Education, and Mr. Yao Zhong-da, Deputy Director, Bureau of Worker and Peasant Education, Ministry of Education for making my participation in the first ICAE study of worker-peasant education in China possible. I would especially like to thank my colleagues on the study team and those "front-liners" working in the area of adult education in China, particularly Messrs. Wang Jian Tiang and Wang Yian-Wei for their human and intellectual support throughout our visit. Finally, I would like to thank Susan Pepper, Richard Skolnick, Ping Chin, Edward Worthy, Halsey Bemer, Peter Seybolt, Mats Hultin, and Leo Orleans for their helpful comments on the original manuscript.

3. Methodologically, the paper is based on four sources of data: field observations and individual interviews conducted during a twenty-four day study mission to the PRC /2; on-site program briefs distributed during visits to major institutions of worker-peasant education, e.g. factories, communes, local government, etc. (see Appendix B); notes taken during symposiums or large group exchanges composed of a cross-section of adult educators and especially organized by the Chinese for the study team; and a review of the relevant literature on Chinese adult education.

4. It should be cautioned that expertise is not something that can be readily acquired in a brief visit to a country as vast and complex as China. Not only was the study team's time in the country short, it was complicated by the necessity to work through interpreters. Some basic principles guided all site visits. First, the Study Team not only heard and read about adult education programs, but also observed such programs being implemented. Secondly, the team was not only exposed to achievements and successes but also to problems and failures. And thirdly, the Team derived data not only from the producers of adult education programs but also from the users of such programs./3

5. The paper is organized to note progress from a brief historical overview and discussion of the Chinese definition and conceptualization of worker-peasant education to an examination of worker-peasant educational organization, policies, and objectives. These sections are followed by a description and analysis of major worker-peasant educational institutions and programs. The paper concludes with a discussion of more general issues and lessons emerging from the Chinese experience in adult education.

/2 The primary data for this paper emanates from participation on the first study team visiting China under the auspices of the China-International Council for Adult Education (ICAE) Cooperation Project. The visit took place from March 15-April 14, 1981 (see Appendix A). The study team was hosted by the Bureau of Worker-Peasant Education, Ministry of Education. The study team members were: Ms. Nita Barrow, primary health care specialist, Barbados; Ms. Kasama Varavang, literacy and adult education specialist, Thailand; Mr. John Whitehouse, Labor Education Specialist, ILO, Canada; Mr. Harry Campbell, media specialist, ICAE, Canada; and Mr. Nat Colletta, Nonformal-Adult Education Specialist, East Asia and Pacific Projects Department, World Bank. The visit was part of a three-year effort to promote the exchange of persons and knowledge on adult education between the Peoples' Republic of China and the sixty plus national adult education associations of the International Council for Adult Education.

/3 The statistics gathered during our field visits should be taken as approximates at best. As Orleans (1974) has observed, "the fact that the Chinese are well known for their talent in mathematics and other sciences should not be confused with their deficiencies in statistics." Most statistics provided to the study team were of achievements and therefore positive in nature. It was extremely difficult to obtain cost data due to the complex mixture of in-kind and currency inputs, as well as to the localized, diverse methods of financing worker-peasant education in China.

Historical Overview of Worker-Peasant Education

6. Though Chinese civilization developed written language over 4,000 years ago, it remained, along with other forms of specialized knowledge, largely the property of a small ruling class. The Confucian period of traditional education exemplified the elitist nature of education in its selection and ideological preparation of future governing elites. Theory ruled supreme over application as there was a general disdain for manual labor and natural science. Up until the time of the first revolutionary activities of the early 1900s, the traditional education system remained an unchallenged mechanism for reproducing the stratified semi-feudalistic society characteristic of ancient China (Lofstedt, 1980).

7. In the early 1920s, apart from efforts to eliminate the examination system, at least two other major challenges to the traditional elitist system of Chinese education were launched by massoriented adult education programs. One was led by anti-government Communist Party leadership and the other by non-governmental Chinese Christian leadership.

8. Borrowing heavily from the revolutionary experience of the Soviet Union, the Communist Party established the first workers' continuing education school in January 1922 at Wufuxiang, Anyuan County, in Jiangxi Province. This was fundamentally a continuing education program held in the evening for railway workers. Jiangxi was one of the first "Central Soviets" or so-called "liberated areas" set up under the leadership of the Chinese Communist Party. In 1923, Mao Zedong established a "self-study university" in Changsha, Hunan Province. Reflecting his personal criticism of formal university study, the university took as its motto, "read by oneself; ponder by oneself; mutually discuss and study," and required no entrance examination (Hawkins, 1973).

9. A few years later, Mao revealed his now famous "Report of an Inspection of the Hunan Peasant Movement" which reported the opening of a number of "village peasant schools." These early Communist-led efforts at mass education focused on raising the "cultural" (literacy level) of the masses combined with providing ideological training. Yao (1980) recounted the success of these early Communist-inspired mass educational activities as follows:

> According to partial statistics from the Central Soviet areas in Jiangxi, Fujian and Guangdong for 1933, some 6,462 continuing education night schools were being operated in 2,932 villages, with an enrollment of 94,517. There were also 32,388 literacy classes being held with an attendance of 155,371. Of these, according to statistics from Xingguo County, women accounted for 69% of the enrollment in the continuing education schools and 60% in the literacy classes.

10. From the mid-1930s to the point of liberation in 1949, the Communist efforts at mass adult education centered and flourished in Mao's revolutionary retreat of Yenan and other border regions and base areas. As Seybolt (1971) and Seldon (1971), among others, point out, there were a variety of educational programs introduced during the Yenan period, e.g. the Chinese People's Anti-Japanese Military and Political College (Kang-ta), the Lu Hsun Academy of Literature and Arts, the Bethune Medical School, the Chinese Women's University, informal reading circles and study criticism groups, among other "mass line" oriented education which "created an important legacy of ideas and innovative practices destined for subsequent revival" (Lucas, 1976).

11. In Yenan, early efforts at popular education and ideological training primarily through evening general literacy classes were soon integrated with social and economic innovations, such as cooperatives, into a comprehensive program to build new socio-economic structures and inculcate appropriate collectivist values among the masses in the newly liberated areas. Evening schools for workers and peasant, half-day schools, winter schools, among other activities of adult education, emerged as early institutional forms. Undergirded by the concept of Minban or Minban gongzhu (management by the people with government assistance), these early revolutionary mass education programs were the roots of many of the worker-peasant education programs of the Great Leap Forward and Cultural Revolution eras.

12. During the Anti-Japanese period (1937-45), adult education reached its highest point. At that time, in the liberated areas the general education policy was that "cadre education was more important than mass education and adult education was more important than children's education" (Yao, 1981).

13. While the Communist Party-led attempts of mass-oriented adult education were being developed in Yenan and in other emerging liberated areas under the guidance of the CPP (with broader influence from the earlier Soviet Revolutionary mass education model), a separate but parallel experiment in mass adult education was evolving in Tinghsien, Hopeh Province. Known as the Mass Education Movement, this movement was guided by James Yen and Tao Xingzhi, a Western-educated, Christian-influenced Chinese who, like his Communist-Marxist-Lenninist influenced counterpart, Mao Zedong, sought to release the masses from the shackles of ignorance and impoverishment (Tao, 1927). In 1923, the Chinese National Association of the Mass Education Movement was organized based on the previous experimental Mass Education Movement activities, some of which, particularly in the area of literacy, actually find their roots in earlier YMCA-assisted efforts to educate Chinese laborers in France during World War I. Its stated purpose was "to explore the potentialities of the masses, and find a way of educating them, not merely for life, but to remake life" (Yen, 1934).

14. This association had representation from twenty provinces and was organized with an Executive Board of nine members and a National Board

composed of two representatives from each province. The Movement gained such momentum that in 1926 the Kiangsu Government at Nanking invited the Movement to form the first Mass Education College in China to train leaders for mass education. A Division of Social Education with responsibility for literacy and adult education was established in the Ministry of Education, and a Bureau of Mass Education was formed, at least on paper, in every hsien (county). This organization was likely the institutional forerunner of the current Bureau of Worker-Peasant Education.

15. At first, the Movement stressed literacy based upon a method developed by Yen called the 1,000 character method. Selecting characters from the spoken language of the people rather than the classical written language of scholars, the "peoples' thousand character texts" (P'ing Min Ch'ien Tsu K'o) were prepared and disseminated by the Movement. In 1929, the Movement shifted from the extensive promotion of literacy to a more intensive study of rural life in an attempt to integrate literacy into broader efforts at community development, e.g. cultural, economic, health, and political sectors. Like the Communists, the Movement viewed the cooperative as being the key institutional mechanism for transforming traditional socio-economic relations.

16. Another important attempt at rural reconstruction through adult education was the founding of the Peasant Movement Training Institute in 1924 under the Kuomintang Government. The Institute was heavily subscribed to by local Communists in Hunan and, as Schram (1966) pointed out, nearly forty percent of the total enrollment was recruited by the Hunan Provincial branch of the party, including Mao's brother.

17. For both Communist and Christian-led mass adult education experiments in revolutionary China, adult education was viewed as an instrument of socio-economic transformation. Its goal was not only to raise the literacy level of the masses but also to change the role of the educational structure itself from one that reconstructed the existing social order of oppression and inequality to one that "dared construct a new social order." However, the degree to which these movements actually challenged the existing structure varies considerably with Mao's efforts manifested in armed struggle while Yen's approach basically supported the existing status quo, albeit from a critical posture.

18. One cannot overlook the probable influence of early progressive American educators, such as John Dewey (who visited China from 1919-23) on the individuals and forces at play during this early period of Chinese revolutionary fervor and educational experimentation (Sizer, 1966). Yen captures the influence and vision of the moment: "This program which we have been working out in China is the program that is needed now for the three-fourths of the world's people, because it is a program for reconstruction which can be carried out by the people themselves. They will become educated as they reconstruct their own lives. It is education through reconstruction and reconstruction through education" (Buck, 1945).

19. Knowledge was to be applied and shared among the masses to improve the life of all citizenry. Education was to be a liberating experience and the agent of subsequent societal democratization. The confluence of theory and practice into action was the essence of the learning experience. Literacy and learning in general were to be inextricably tied to broader social change.

20. It is hard to say just how much these two major early movements of Chinese adult education were in direct communication. There is no record of personal exchanges between Mao and Yen although it is known that the Communists, including Mao, praised Yen's colleague Tao Xingzhi (Chinese Education, 1974). However, Schram (1966), commenting on "Mao's genius for exploiting respectable people and institutions for radical ends," observed that Mao guided the Hunan program of the Mass Education Movement but "instead of using the textbooks employed elsewhere, Mao had a special set prepared." These texts stressed class conflict and Communism. Later, we will trace other relationships in the adult education programs of revolutionary China under Mao and the earlier Yen experiment.

21. In 1947, when the Mass Education Movement had turned for support to the Chang Kai-Shek Nationalist Government and was clearly associated with "negative" foreign missionary and American aid influences, Yen was forced to flee the mainland, first operating on Taiwan and later internationalizing his mass education program in the present day International Rural Reconstruction Movement headquartered in the Philippines.

22. The first National Conference on Workers' and Peasants' Education convened in September 1950. Soon after, "short-term middle schools" for workers and "winter schools" for peasants were institutionalized as major programs to eliminate illiteracy in coordination with land reform and production efforts. During the early 1950s, eradicating illiteracy or "raising the cultural level" of the masses dominated the adult education scene. While mass campaigns were launched earlier in some parts of the country, they only began to spread throughout the country during the 1950s. In the beginning of the mass literacy campaigns in 1952, the so-called "quick method" was developed (probably based on Yen's earlier literacy technique) in an attempt to reduce the learning period from three years to three hundred hours by focusing on phonetic symbols. Literacy became an important tool for realizing revolutionary and ideological consolidation.

23. In 1953, with the adoption of the Stalinist-type economic development strategy of the first five-year plan (1953-57) in which priority was placed on capital intensive industrial development, the concept of sparetime education to upgrade the skill level of workers took precedence over mass peasant education. Sparetime education was designed to provide the requisite skilled labor pool for the shifting emphasis to industrialization. Much of the worker education programming which is now emerging under the "four modernization" program had its roots in this early period of adult education for rapid industrial development (1955-1958). We

will return to discuss this era in greater detail under "enterprise" education.

24. The 1949-58 period of adult education was, at least statistically, notably successful. By 1958, upon the dawning of the "Great Leap Forward," the following results were proclaimed (Orleans, 1960):

SPARETIME AND ILLITERATE STUDENTS, 1949-58
(in thousands)

Year	In spare-time higher schools	In spare-time secondary all schools	In spare-time secondary schools	In spare-time primary schools	In anti-illiteracy classes
1949	0.1	0.1	-	-	657.07
1950	0.4	0.1	-	-	1,372.0
1951	1.6	0.3	-	-	1,375.0
1952	4.2	0.7	249.0	1,375.0	656.0
1953	9.7	1.1	404.0	1,523.0	2,954.0
1954	13.2	186.0	760.0	2,088.0	2,637.0
1955	15.9	195.0	1,167.0	4,538.0	3,678.0
1956	63.8	563.0	2,236.0	5,195.0	7,434.0
1957	75.9	588.0	2,714.0	6,267.0	7,208.0
1958	150.0	-	5,000.0	26,000.0	40,000.0

Blanks indicate figures are not available.

Source: Ten Great Years (Peking: State Statistical Bureau, 1960).

One might conjecture that the lack of available aggregate data on sparetime education during the "Great Leap Forward" era (1959-66) may be indicative of a more general decline in adult education activities similar to what transpired in formal education due to economic failures (Hultin, 1981).

25. Despite its positive results in the adult education arena, the first five-year plan led to a number of imbalances and contradictions, e.g. between industry and agriculture, between capital-intensive and labor-intensive modes of production, and between large-scale and small-scale development strategies culminating in the "Great Leap Forward" of 1958-61. Initially, the "Great Leap Forward" endeavored to rectify these imbalances through industrial decentralization and the transformation of the cooperative movement into the commune movement, e.g. consolidation of cooperatives into larger-scale communes which could support sideline or rural industries producing for local consumption.

Mismanagement and poor weather, coupled with the worsening of Soviet-Chinese relations, opened a larger ideological debate of "Redness" versus "Expertness". The economic failures of the first five-year plan and the ensuing attempts at instant remedy through the Great Leap Forward laid the foundation for a paralyzing Chinese self-doubt which provided the basis for the Cultural Revolution.

26. From the stress on ideological consolidation via literacy promotion among the masses of the early 1950s, to the emphasis on more specialized skill-oriented sparetime education for workers in factories, and scientific agriculturalists on communes of the mid-1950s and early 1960s, the Chinese came full circle back to a revolutionary and ideological emphasis on adult education during the Cultural Revolution (1966-76) period. Factory sparetime schools became "July 21 Workers Universities" and commune sparetime agrotechnical schools became "May 7 Peasant Agricultural Colleges" with ideological training prevailing over the transmission of technical and scientific skills.

27. As Barendson (1975) summarized:

> Thus the main thrust of his (Mao's) educational policy since 1949 has been to produce a new type of intelligentsia by making the necessary general and specialized education available to politically reliable working class elements and insisting that all students be required to receive regular political education in schools and participate regularly in manual labor as part of the school program.

28. The major directive for the "May 7 Cadre Schools" linking education in the army, factories and communes to that of formal schools emanates from the Mao's May 7, 1966 letter to Lin Piao which is summarized by Chen (1974) as follows:

> The letter (from Mao) to Lin Piao was concerned with the army and instructed that the PLA 'should be a great school' in which 'the armymen should learn politics, military affairs, and agriculture,' and 'take part in the socialist education movement in the factories and villages.' The army should engage in three major tasks: 'agriculture, industry, and mass work.' After these specific instructions for the army, Mao's letter went on to apply his ideas to education in general, stressing the importance of 'learning other things.' Workers and peasants should study 'military affairs, politics, and culture' and engage in criticizing the bourgeoisie. Students should 'learn other things, that is, industrial work, farming, and military affairs. They should also criticize the bourgeoisie.' The same principle holds for government and Party personnel and for people in trade and commerce. The section on students includes Mao's often repeated statements on the need to shorten the school term and terminate the domination of the schools by bourgeois intellectuals.

29. As for the July 21 Workers Universities, the experience at Shanghai Machine Tool Plant, where technicians and workers were trained in workshops and classes by veteran workers and equated to university graduates, formed the basis of Mao's July 21, 1968 directive:

> It is still necessary to have universities; here I refer mainly to colleges of science and engineering. However, it is essential to shorten the length of schooling, revolutionize education, put proletarian politics in command, and follow the road of the Shanghai Machine Tool Plant in training technicians from among the workers. Students should be selected from among workers and peasants with practical experience and they should return to production work after a few years of study (Barendson, 1974).

30. The July 21 Workers Universities and May 7 Cadre Schools were complemented by a "rustification" program which involved the forced transfer of students and intellectuals to the countryside to expose those with "revisionist" ideas to the ideological tenets of the Socialist State through re-education and manual labor./4 As the issue of succession to Mao's leadership gained prominence over the earlier debate of the choice of an appropriate development strategy, adult education, particularly in the above-mentioned forms of the Cultural Revolution, became a messianic movement for the ideological purification of earlier intellectual and technocratic sinners.

31. Finally, with the downfall of the Gang of Four and the official end to the Cultural Revolution (1976), the Chinese were left in a state referred to as the "three lows and one lack," e.g. low cultural level, low technical standard, low ability of management, and a lack of engineers and technicians. An economic development strategy is now emerging which has swung the ideological pendulum toward the right in an attempt to balance scientific agriculture with industry, to have a mixture of scale, to create a complementarity of socialist and capitalist incentive systems, and, ultimately, to blend the development of worker and peasant education and formal and adult education into a unified system of education and training with equivalent standards, quality, certification, incentives and legitimacy. However, many China scholars would claim that the new swing right has merely ushered back an elitest, urban biased intellectual and cadre class.

/4 At least in form, rustification was tried under the Mass Education Movement in 1929. The leading Peking Newspaper reported at that time: "It was the most magnificient exodus of the intelligentsia into the country that had taken place in Chinese History to date. Holders of old imperial degrees, professors of national universities, a college president and a number of Ph.D's and M.D.s from leading American Universities had left their positions and comfortable homes in cities to go to the backwoods of Tinghsun to find ways and means to revitalize the life of an ancient, backward people, and to build democracy from the bottom up" (Mass Education Movement Report 1944). However, it should be noted that this was a "voluntary" program of rural service.

...al conditions have changed so too have the socio-economic de... ...strategies and attendant educational modes, content emphasis, administrative control, and nomenclatures. In many parts of the country functional substitutes for July 21 Workers Universities, May 7 Peasant Agricultural Colleges, and other innovative adult education programs of the Cultural Revolution are now beginning to revert to their earlier pre-Cultural Revolution names of Workers Sparetime Universities and Agrotechnical Sparetime Schools. For example, at the Zhujinbu People's Commune sparetime agrotechnical school, the school was formally called a May 7 Peasant Agricultural College, but the name was recently changed after the fall of the Gang of Four to acknowledge the "appropriate" standard or level and to dissassociate it from the Gang of Four. This has been accompanied by a substantive shift in curriculum from ideological to technical content and administrative control from inexperienced revolutionary ideologues to the old revolutionary cadre and intellectual vanguard of the 1950s. Financing has remained primarily a local, factory or commune, matter; however, the central government has recently taken a more active hand in forming policy, setting standards, and monitoring quality.

33. Ideological-oriented adult educational programs such as the May 7 Cadre Schools and the student and intellectual rustification programs have been either abolished and/or are rapidly winding down. Literacy efforts, which generally were largely dormant during the Cultural Revolution, are now being reconstituted mainly through sparetime upper primary schools and evening classes for adults. From parallel and competing systems, the formal school and adult education programs of the Cultural Revolutionary Period and are now being viewed as integrated and complementary programs under a single education and training system. The Government's goal is to institutionalize and systematize "all education to serve the National Development Goals of the "Four Modernizations" - Industry, Agriculture, the Army, Science and Technology." As summarized by Yao (1981), Deputy Director of the Bureau for Worker-Peasant Education: "China is under a period of restoration; during the Cultural Revolution adult education was destroyed." This may have, in fact ultimately been true, but it is somewhat misleading in that early on the Cultural Revolution strongly supported many innovations in Adult Education.

34. The above brief historical overview sets the stage for understanding the present concept, organization, policies, and objectives of worker-peasant education in the Peoples' Republic of China. These historical roots will be elaborated on in later discussions of the major institutions and programs of worker-peasant education now under restoration in China.

Worker-Peasant Education: Concept, Organization, Policies, and Objectives

35. Mr. Yao (1981) opened a discussion on the Chinese concept of adult education by quoting Tao Xingzhi, a former student of John Dewey, on

education: "life is education, society is school." He was making the distinction between informal, nonformal, and formal education.

> For the Chinese, education takes place in the home (family), society, and the school, with societal education including such informal educational activities as films, libraries, museums, and the arts. In China, adult education belongs to school education, the level of literacy, culture and knowledge is quite the same as in the formal schools. Adult education is supplemental and a continuation of formal schooling - nonformal education belongs to the realm of societal education (Yao, 1981)./5.

Although there is considerable difference, especially in quality, adult education in China is currently viewed as school equivalency. The primary differences between what the Chinese refer to as sparetime schools and the regular age-graded schools are: client population, administrative sponsorship, and financial resource.

36. While adult education prior to and during the Cultural Revolution may have connoted the full range of teaching-learning experiences outside of the normal age-graded school system, frequently referred to as non-formal education, today the Chinese are vigorously trying to systematize and institutionalize such exchanges into a school-like model and concept for raising the cultural (literacy), scientific, and technological levels of workers and peasants. As Yao (1981) historically summarized, "we inherited poor quality schools and intellectuals from the old society at the time of independence. We established specific schools and courses for workers and peasants, calling on factories and communes to run spare time courses. This tradition lasted through the 1950s and early 1960s. We are now restoring some of the good points from this period."

37. The overall structure of worker-peasant education is well established (see Appendix C). At the apex is the Bureau of Worker-Peasant Education, Ministry of Education. The Bureau is organized into three principal Divisions: Worker Education, Peasant Education and Correspondence Education. The primary function of the Bureau is to understand problems

---

/5 James Yen (1934) and Tao Xhingzhi (1927) made similar educational modal distinctions as follows: "the school type operates in three kinds of schools: the primary schools, the people's schools [literacy classes], and the Farmers' Institute [roughly equivalent to agrotechnical sparetime schools, yet omitting workers sparetime schools and universities since Yen's was essentially a rural-based program]; the social type which is directed particularly at the graduates of the peoples' schools, who are organized into 'alumni associations' for self-education and community improvement; and the home type which aims at socializing the home in order to make it an effective educative force for reconstruction, and is directed particularly at the young women."

through investigation (research), provide policy planning advice to the Central Committee, set standards and exams, produce core curriculum, monitor quality,/6 and oversee the implementation of policy throughout the country. In undertaking the above tasks the Bureau provides a standard setting and quality control function for the Nation's overall program in worker-peasant education. There are similar divisions and sections of the Bureau of Worker-Peasant Education at the Province and County levels (see Appendices C and D), respectively, performing parallel functions and serving as the implementation arms of the National Level Bureau. At the rural commune, urban municipality, and production enterprise levels, e.g., production teams, neighborhoods, workshops, there are a plurality of organizational arrangements for adult education. This variety of lower level organizations reflects both the diversity of learner needs and the decentralized nature of the administration and funding of adult education (see Appendix E, Brigade level sparetime education organization).

38. Along with the vertical administrative arrangements from the National Ministry of Education to the commune level, there are also a set of horizontal Worker-Peasant Education Coordinating Committees at each geo-political level with representation from a variety of agencies, e.g. Ministry of Trade, All China Federation of Workers, Communist Youth League, etc./7 The primary function of such coordinating bodies is to ensure the interface of individual programs of various agencies, coordinate planning and policy formation, and the exchange of experiences, and generally oversee the implementing institutions, e.g., factories, communes, implementing programs.

/6 It is interesting to observe the great stress being placed on the poor quality of "college education" offered to the masses during the Cultural Revolution and the need to upgrade college graduates from that era. For example, according to Yao (1981), among the 500,000 students in various kinds of college level sparetime education in Beijing at this time, there are an estimated 50,000 who had previously received a higher education program during the Cultural Revolution. However good intentioned such upgrading may be, it is fair to say that it also offers a ready opportunity to resocialize youth to the new party line under the guise of upgrading the poor quality education they obtained in May 7 and July 21 peasants and workers colleges. Even the Medical College of Beijing is currently conducting a two year T.V. course for those students who graduated from medical schools during the Cultural Revolution, about 24,000 students in all (discussion with the Provost of the Medical Training College of Beijing, 1981).

/7 The membership of the coordinating body are: Leading enterprises; All China Federation of Workers; National Federation of Women; Departments of Defense, Labor, Agriculture, Health, Finance and Trade, and Education; Science and Technology, Construction, Industry, Economic Commission, Mass Media (news and broadcast); and Communist Youth League and Party.

39. While adult education is led by the Government, particularly the Bureau for Worker-Peasant Education, the actual programming and implementation is with the cooperation of a range of mass organizations, communes, municipalities, and enterprises. This has resulted in the following major diverse institutional forms of adult education delivery and use. First, the regular school system conducts sparetime, evening, and correspondence educational programs for adults. These are typically certificate-granting school equivalency programs at the primary, secondary, or university levels. These programs are similar to the standard continuing education programs of North American institutions of learning and are not the focus of this paper. Secondly, enterprises, usually in cooperation with the labor unions, run sparetime upper primary, secondary, and university parallel educational programs as well as in-service technical courses for employee upgrading. Thirdly, the rural communes, inclusive of production brigades and teams, offer sparetime school equivalency programs at primary and secondary levels, along with specialized agrotechnical and managerial courses for the preparation of agricultural technicians. Fourthly, the local governments, e.g. municipal and district governments, conduct sparetime secondary and university education programs. Fifthly, a number of mass organizations, primarily the labor unions, women's federation, and youth league, provide mobilizational and instructional (and sometimes financial) support to constituencies for sparetime education programs. Finally, the Central Television and Broadcasting University (with local affiliates) conduct sparetime educational programming often in conjunction with enterprises and others for viewing.

40. There are primarily three adult learning production-linked instructional modes: full-time in which employees are released with full pay and benefits for a period of time from six months to three years to acquire new knowledge and skills; part-time which is a form of in-service training typically amounting to short term courses and apprenticeships of varying lengths; and sparetime which is about four to six hours each week and suppplemental to one's normal productive role and activities as will be seen in subsequent detailed discussions of the major adult education institutions, e.g., enterprises, communes, municipalities (local government), and major mass organizations. All such institutions offer these three learning production-linked instructional modes.

41. While it was impossible to obtain aggregate numbers on the actual users, the potential users of these programs represent a population of approximately 600 million adults, consisting of approximately 400 million peasants, 100 million workers, and an additional 100 million cadre (government officials, management, and in a general sense "leaders" of all types and levels). The age of the users is from 14 to 40 years old, although people over 40 are not necessarily excluded from participation in such adult education programs. Priority, however, is given to those in the 14-40 age group.

42. Staff members for adult education are either professional full-time adult educators (estimated at 3-5 teachers for every 5,000 students) and part-time or "visiting" teachers. The visiting teachers are either fulltime teachers in the formal education system and/or technical and professional persons who double as teachers of their specific expertise along with performing their regular work roles.

43. Curricula for these programs are based on a combination of nationally and locally produced (by enterprise, local government, or commune) instructional materials. There are basically five types of instructional materials: (1) literacy textbooks compiled by the province; (2) textbooks for sparetime primary and new literates courses compiled by the Ministry of Education or the provincial education organs; (3) textbooks for junior or middle schools compiled by the Ministry of Education; (4) textbooks of basic agricultural knowledge compiled by specialists in agriculture and sideline occupations; and (5) textbooks for staff and workers' education compiled by the Ministry of Education, enterprises, and other concerned production units. There is currently a move afoot to further standardize the core curricula for various programs in line with regular formal school curricula; however, the Central Government continues to encourage the development of local materials to supplement standardized curricula in order to make instruction more relevant to local conditions and needs.

44. Finance of adult education is a complex matter since it is a mixture of local (production unit) and state financing. Funds usually come from direct contributions of the masses through: (a) brigade, commune, workshop, and factory channels in accordance with their respective financial power and the principle of self-reliance; (b) mass organizations like the All China Federation of Workers; and (c) direct financing from the State (usually allocated for the training of teachers, meetings, printing and distributing instructional materials, and praising oustanding efforts). It is noteworthy that individuals either through small fees for books or labor exchange contribute more to the financing of their own education than one might have expected in a Socialist system. Actual costs will be discussed under each major adult education institutional program.

45. Policy-making in the area of adult education involves four key steps: (a) basic investigation; (b) a national conference to discuss findings (models and problems); (c) formulation of policy at the Central Committee level; and (d) popularization of policy directives which includes the promotion of models and the criticism of failures. Planning, as opposed to policy formulation, is usually done through a process of descent and ascent through the bureaucratic levels - from the Central Committee down to the production brigade-team committees and back up.

46. Planning adult education has to be seen within the context of the Nation's broader five-year policy and plans as set out by the then Minister of Education Mr. Liu Xiyao at the April 22, 1978 National Education

Conference. He stated that there are four guiding principles for educational development in China for the period 1978-1985. These are:

> (a) revolutionizing education; (b) structuring educational outputs to the needs and capabilities of China's economic development; (c) adjusting the content and methodology of teaching to the demands of modern science and technology; and (d) placing greater stress on raising the quality of education, especially higher education's ability to produce skilled personnel (Hershede, 1979).

It should be noted that higher education in the Chinese context includes sparetime university equivalency training operated through the T.V. University in enterprises and by local Municipal and District sparetime education institutions along with regular university-based formal education programs.

47. Proceeding from the general National Educational guiding principles of the sixth five-year plan, Zang Boping (1980), Vice-Minister for Education responsible for worker-peasant education outlined the following objectives for the role of adult education in socialist modernization:

> Firstly, the intensification of adult education to increase the rate of labor productivity; secondly, to augment and renew scientific and technical knowledge of a work force that has basically been out of touch with recent developments in their fields and professions; thirdly, the intensification of adult education as a major avenue for training specialists in the various trades and industries such as engineering technicians, agricultural and livestock specialists, management specialists of all kinds, teachers, doctors, etc.; fourthly, to build the cultural level, that is to say the general educational level, necessary for a highly socialist cultural civilization.

48. Emphasis is placed on the need to consider general and adult education in an equal and integrated fashion. As Vice Minister Zang Boping (1980) summarized: "We must smash the traditional view that general education is superior to adult education, cast aside the narrow viewpoint that education and output stand in opposition to each other, and vigorously intensify adult education work." He proceeded to call for every commune and productive enterprise to have an education plan for developing adult education and that the employment and remuneration of people who participate in such sparetime programs should be equivalent to that received by formal school graduates following testing and certification.

49. From the preceding discussion, it can be clearly seen that the Chinese have taken the potential role of adult education in the modernization process seriously. The current emphasis on worker education comes in response to an identified need to upgrade worker skills and general educational background:

In terms of cultural knowledge and professional skills, according to a late 1979 survey of two million staff and workers, 80% had not reached a junior middle cultural level, and 7.8 percent were illiterate or semiliterate. Real worker operating skills were low, and most were below grade 2 technical level; managerial personnel generally lacked modern industrial management expertise; technicians accounted for only 2.8 percent of all staff and workers in industrial agencies, and many of these had received no college level education. A lack of skills was a universal problem. If these circumstances were not altered, modern construction cannot be properly conducted, and in order to alter them staff and worker education must be vigorously developed" (Yuan Baohu, 1980)./8

50. The specific targets set for the sixth five-year plan in an attempt to alter these circumstances described by Yuan Boahu are ambitious to say the least. They are:

(a) To provide in-service education through adult education for all workers by 1985. Over one million workers will undergo at least one short-term training in rotation. This should be especially possible since the current plans for industrial restructuring should free up parts of the work force for adult education.

(b) To raise from 60% to 80% (by 1985) the cultural level of those workers below middle-school level to that level by 1985. One-third of those at middle school level must be brought up to senior school level, and all those at senior levels must be raised to college level.

(c) To upgrade the management skills of the most important leadership cadre in business and industry.

(d) To raise the skill level of youth and adult workers by one or two grades so that there will be an increase in the number of technical workers at the secondary and middle school levels by 1985.

(e) In addition to enterprise cadre and worker education targets, staff and worker education may also include upgrading of professional departments (civil service) and mass organizations, among other bodies.

/8 Slightly differing figures are reported in Hultin's study (1981): factory illiteracy rate - 5%; 70% of the labor force had less than 6-7 years schooling (junior secondary); and most of the 20-30% of those with junior secondary education (up to 70% in some industries) had received a poor quality education during the Cultural Revolution period.

51. The stress on worker education is obviously a result of the quest to realize a modern Chinese State. This should not be interpreted as an outright dismissal of peasant education. In fact, in the rural areas literacy efforts are now being combined with primary school development to attack the estimated 30-35 percent illiteracy rate - most illiterates are in rural areas - and many are minorities, i.e. particularly pastoral nomads. In addition to basic education, increased opportunities for secondary education will be offered through sparetime commune, municipal, and enterprise run secondary schools. Agricultural education is shifting to "scientific" agrotechnical training in sparetime agrotechnical secondary schools and through specialized short agrotechnical courses as the Chinese seek to modernize the agricultural sector as well as the urban industrial sector.

52. The 1979 National Congress on Peasant Education issued a policy statement on peasant education directing the spread of secondary and technical education to peasants through sparetime and evening schools, broadcasting for agriculture, and various short-term training classes. The short-term training includes travelling demonstrations of new agricultural techniques and mobile exhibitions on science and technology.

53. Herschede (1979) observed that "in sum, the educational framework now being set up is reminiscent of the one established between the Great Leap Forward, 1958-1959, and the Cultural Revolution, 1966-1969. It is essentially a multi-track system that offers Chinese planners a spectrum of school sizes and alternative forms of instruction." One could add that the present thrust also draws heavily from the pre-Great Leap Forward period (1955-58) as well as from Mass Education Programs between 1922 and 1949.

54. Understanding the general concept, organization, policy, and objectives of worker-peasant education is a useful introduction to the enormity of the task which Chinese adult educators have set for themselves. Despite Lucas' (1976) warning that "the full range of adult education forms [in China] defies any succinct characterization," it may be helpful to examine the major adult education institutions and programs in a more in-depth manner in order to comprehend China's general capacity for realizing its goals of worker-peasant education. These major adult education institutions and programs will be described in terms of these general characteristics: major clientele or target group, program objective, techniques for popularizing the program (motivating participation), general organization and administration, curriculum, instructional methods, teaching-learning materials, staffing, cost and financing, and monitoring and evaluation.

Major Institutions and Programs of Worker-Peasant Education

Enterprises (Worker Education)

55. A main goal of the Chinese Revolution has been an attempt to eliminate the distinction between worker performance tasks and management administrative functions, between manual labor and intellectual labor, and ultimately between town and countryside. The key concepts of worker management, production-linked education, and sideline or small-scale industrial development in the context of communes have been directly aimed at blending and, ultimately, eliminating these distinctions. Most factories or enterprises have at one time or another organized schools where workers could obtain new skills and knowledge, upgrade existing skills, and prepare for new roles and functions.

56. As indicated previously, accompanying the first five-year industrial-oriented plan, efforts were made to introduce a variety of training schemes for workers within factories. The concept of workers sparetime schools had its strongest roots during this industrialization drive of the mid- and late-1950s. As historically acknowledged by the Director of the Peking Second Cotton Mill, "with the development of production, we opened a staff and workers' sparetime school since the operation started in 1955. At that time, there were over 5,000 workers. Most of them only went to primary school. Some were illiterate or semiliterate so the task of staff and workers' education was focused on popularizing junior middle schooling and eliminating illiteracy." In the mid-1950s as progress was being made on the literacy front emphasis shifted more and more to technical training.

57. With the Great Leap Forward and the attempt to reduce disparities between worker and management, city and farm, and industry and agriculture came the "two participations" whereby workers participated in management and managers took part in line production. Emanating from the Ashan Constitution (1960), this plan expanded worker education from the literacy training of the early 1950s, through the skill training emphasis of the mid-1950s, to the world of worker control of the 1960s as "politics took command" (Bettelheim, 1974).

58. At the advent of the Cultural Revolution, sparetime factory schools became July 21 Workers Universities as "serving the people" replaced the goal of professional advancement, ideology replaced scientific competence, and adult education became highly politicized. In sum, political goals replaced production targets as politics, indeed, took command.

59. To address the distinction between manual and intellectual work, the "three in one" concept was introduced; joint management teams of workers, technicians, and cadres (managers) were formed to break down the existing division of labor and to reorganize work relations in factories. Such teams primarily provided ideological training, but experiences were also created which exposed engineers to manual work and technicians to engineering and manual labor and placed workers in direct management or leadership roles. In

addition, May 7 Cadre Schools were established in the countryside. These schools served the dual function of manifestly providing an institutional arrangement for the ideological purification of factory management and leadership (cadre with revisionist tendencies) through manual labor while latently providing managerial and technical skills for industrializing the rural areas, thus bridging the gap between town and countryside. In some instances, the development of many sideline commune industries was stimulated in this fashion. However, even earlier, during the Great Leap Forward era (1958-1959), industries with sparetime schools were "directed to train personnel in the many small or newly established commune industries. The industrial plants complied by sending teachers to classes organized in the new or smaller factories, or by arranging for the scattered workers to attend expanded classes in the major plants" (Harper, 1964).

60. Factory Extension. In addition to creating the July 21 Workers Universities within enterprises and the May 7 Cadre Schools - latently linked to the emergence of rural industry - there was a general effort to decentralize industry in the urban areas by encouraging neighborhood committees to set up collective small-scale enterprises or "street factories." Most of these industries were started by women seeking additional family income and more liberating roles, and producing for the local consumer, e.g. soap, sewing, shoe and other repair operations (Bettleheim, 1974).

61. This effort to restructure social and productive relationships led to the development of rural industry as a system of simple networks emerged to link large-scale urban factories to small-scale urban "street factories" and rural commune "sideline industries." In effect, enterprises became an industrial version of American Land Grant Agricultural Colleges or some American Community Colleges as they extended their expertise and technical assistance to neighborhoods and communes to help establish small scale industry. As communes developed the capacity to produce goods which they had previously imported from urban areas, they could better realize their goal of self-reliance. It was hoped that the gradual urbanization of the communes and the ruralization of the large factories through such factory extension education and technical extension programs would hasten the breaking down of distinctions between industry and agriculture, and between city and countryside. On the other hand urban and rural areas became increasingly separated by the prohibitions on free movement between areas.

62. This role of some factories as extension agents and the process by which a factory might perform this role were succinctly described by the Director of Hunan Rubber Factory as follows:

> First we sent several technicians and workers out to Taijing commune to discuss plans for setting up a small workshop to produce rubber boots. We then invited several persons from the commune to come and train by working in our boot production unit. While they were here our staff brought some of our

> extra equipment to the commune and estabished a small workshop. Their trainees in our factory then returned and our technical staff stayed on to help them get going. This whole process took about six months to a year. After an additional few months our staff were able to return to the main factory. As they faced problems in the commune workshop they would call on us and we would help them solve them. When their commune workshop production was at a level whereby they could meet our previous market demand we totally stopped producing that particular line of boot and in effect turned our market over to them and our attention to producing new items (Interview, April 1981).

63. Inplant Sparetime Education. Currently major urban enterprises and rural sideline industries which incorporate contemporary adult education activities offer three general modes of training and education: fulltime relief from production with full pay and benefits; parttime relief from production with full pay and benefits; and sparetime schooling usually after working hours.

64. Those studying fulltime typically do so through the media of T.V. lectures, correspondence courses, and/or classroom work within the plant in university degree equivalent programs. Fulltime programs such as these are geared toward moving technicians to engineer levels. The part-time training mode is usually offered from four to six hours per week but can be up to half time. This program combines classroom training and on-the-job apprenticeships and is focused on technical content to move workers up to the technician level or upgrade technical skills through in-service training. Leadership and management training is also usually conducted in the part-time mode. In some cases, technicians and/or managers are released halftime, up to six months, for more intensive in-service training. The third major mode is sparetime education which is typically provided in-plant but after working hours (three evenings per week for two or three hours each). This is generally a middle or upper secondary school equivalency program. Language studies and other specialized courses may also be offered in this mode, but the factory only covers the costs of those sparetime studies directly related to the production process of the plant.

65. In addition to the above in-plant programs, many enterprises have sent employees to fulltime regular state universities and sparetime colleges run by the local government. For example, at Guangzhou Heavy Machinery Plant, 22 persons have recently been sent to study in regular universities and 155 persons have been enrolled in provincial and municipal sparetime colleges.

66. Administratively, there is a lead education committee in each enterprise composed of representatives from the Party, Plant administration, Workers' Union, Youth League, Women's Federation, and technical departments. They make all first line decisions regarding educational goals, plans,

enrollments, staffing, time schedule, finance, equipment, etc. A director and staff for factory sparetime education is appointed to oversee the implementation of their decisions.

67. <u>Workshop Apprenticeship Training and Basic Education</u>. While the dominant instructional-learning modes, content focus, and target populations of apprenticeship training and basic education activities fall under the general guidance of the plant and, in particular, the Sparetime College Educational Committee, individual workshops within the plants visited by the study team had worker education committees and offered their own sparetime courses. Each workshop has a deputy director in charge of adult education and one technician responsible for specific tutorial activities. The workshop classes comprise mainly literacy or basic education courses. They are provided six hours per week in two hour sessions three days per week.

68. Also, lectures by workshop technicians which focus on specific technical and production related problems are offered for all employees. New workers within the various workshops are usually assigned to lead (master) workers under an apprenticeship arrangement. There are frequent workers' assemblies to air major concerns and plans. Workshops and workshop technicians are heavily involved in on-the-job and apprenticeship training, providing lab facilities and instructional staff respectively. For example, to illustrate the scope of the efforts conducted by workshop units, at Beijing First Cotton Mill primary technical education has developed greatly over the years. According to 1979 statistics, "study classes, technical training in rotation classes, technical practice and operation competitions organized by different workshops have been held more than 980 times, and joined by 260,000 persons" (Plant Brief, 1981).

69. Many of the instructional staff come from neighboring normal colleges or universities or enterprise-administered formal primary and secondary schools. As mentioned before, technical-course staff are regular factory technicians who double as adult education instructors. All instructors are typically paid about six yuan ($4) per instructional hour or are paid in kind, e.g. they are given release time from normal production activities or work points. However, wages generally vary depending on the income of the production unit, e.g., brigades, enterprises.

70. One must remember that most urban enterprises of a large scale are, in effect, cradle-to-grave communities providing all services (including formal schools) and goods to their staff and their families. (Food provision may be the only exception to this self-sufficient, self-constrained aspect of urban enterprises; however, some even cultivate small land areas to provide for partial food requirements.)

71. The facilities of the plant itself, e.g., workshops which may be idle, primary and secondary school classrooms within the plant compound, and in some cases, specially constructed community and/or sparetime education

centers, are utilized for adult education. Equipment, e.g. television, lab instruments, etc., is either that of the workshops or directly purchased by the plant. Instructional materials are regular school and university texts provided by the Bureau of Worker-Peasant Education, supplemented by local enterprise produced manuals, handbooks, and the like. All plants visited by the Study Team had small libraries and/or reading rooms with very modest holdings.

72. The adult education activities of enterprises are financed from four major sources: labor union contributions from workers' wages;/9 direct reinvestment of profits, varying from enterprise to enterprise; a modest state contribution for books and equipment; and direct student fees. The latter category is only for those courses which the factory deems not directly related to the production processes of the plant. Actual unit costs for instruction were difficult to obtain and where such data was available costs were not uniform from one enterprise to another. For example, in Hunan Power Machinery Plant the cost given was 600 Yuan ($400) per student per year (32 weeks, 24 hours per week) for technical courses and secondary equivalence, and 700 yuan ($466) per student per year (20 weeks, 24 hours per week) for T.V. University equivalency courses. The opportunity cost of student labor for the T.V. University equivalency courses was about 40 yuan ($27) (wages) per month, while the opportunity cost of secondary school equivalency was given as zero since students in this program were not on the payroll of the plant. The T.V. University cost only includes the cost to the factory and not of the Central T.V. and Broadcast University. Broadcast costs for Beijing T.V. University, for example, are calculated at approximately 20 yuan ($13) per student per semester. The table in Appendix F presents enrollments, staffing, and cost estimates (where available) in the several factories visited by the Study Team.

73. State owned enterprises are now required to develop sparetime education plans. Such plans are expected to set specific targets in line with meeting the broader goals and objectives set out for worker education in the five year plan. For example, Chengdu Rolling Stock Plant has established a plan with the following specific goals: "By the year 1985, 80 percent of the workers less than 35 years old and with schooling of junior middle school level will be brought up to the equivalent level of that of secondary technical school graduates; also by 1985, all staff member and workers less than 35 will receive a junior middle school education" (Plant Brief, 1981).

74. It is estimated that by 1985 more than half of the needs for middle-level technicians and lower level professionals will be met by workers' universities. The following table provides a picture of recent Worker University enrollment trends (World Bank, 1981):

/9 Trade unions collect 2 percent of the total enterprise employee wages to finance all their activities; e.g. recreation, education, etc. The Central Committee stipulates that 25-30 percent of that 2 percent of total wages be spent on education.

WORKER COLLEGES
(July 21 Worker Colleges)

Years	Number of colleges	Number of students enrolled
1975	1,200	90,000
1976	6,000	460,000
1977	15,000	780,000
1979	-	860,000

Source: Hultin, 1981.

75. While it is difficult to sort out the differential impact of the numerous variables, e.g. technology, training, finance, organization, impacting on the production function of factories, the Chinese usually attribute marked changes in productivity to the adult education program. For example, at the Foshan Silk Textile Factory they attribute a 15 percent excess of planned production, an increase in quality (fewer rejects) of five percent, and profit of 66 percent in excess of that planned to training. At Peking First Cotton Mill, the Director stated that:

> The development of the staff and workers' education has raised their cultural and technical level, and has brought about the advance in production. Now 120,000 cotton yarns are produced each year, which is double that produced in the beginning years of the factory.

Research assessing the comparative cost-benefit analysis of worker education schemes is sorely needed and would likely be welcomed by the Chinese themselves at this time.

76. The Chinese, especially through the activities of the Bureau of Worker-Peasant Education, are now trying to "emulate" or standardize course content, exams, and certification among enterprises. As the Director of the Hunan Rubber Plan stated, "the classes emulate each other in activities of study, in the size of enrollment, in the rate of attendance, in consolidation work, in the passing of exams, and so on." There is little doubt that the ultimate goal is to raise the quality of worker education through academic standardization while keeping financing, administrative control, and accountability in the hands of the local enterprises. The concepts of educational quality and school certification have finally come to the workplace in China.

The Communes (Peasant Education)

77. Like the enterprise workshop, each commune production brigade is now required to produce an annual sparetime education plan. This plan is kept simple typically covering four areas: user needs; study time allocation; staffing of courses and regulations; and a clear statement of rewards, incentives, and measures of performance (exam requirements). Once more, this is in line with the Bureau of Worker-Peasant Education's overriding goal to standardize, certify, and improve the quality of adult education (see sample Brigade Sparetime Education Plan Appendix H).

78. There is also a strong emphasis on consolidating and integrating educational activities: literacy is linked to technology and science, classroom study to practice and production, primary schools to adult education, agrotechnical secondary schools to agrotechnical stations, and commune hospitals and health centers to the training of primary health care workers. There is little doubt that though worker education is receiving higher visibility and media coverage under the "four modernization" policy, peasant education, particularly as it relates to the practice of scientific agriculture, remains of considerable importance. The generic themes of integration and consolidation are clearly guiding economic development principles, balancing political extremes and trade-offs between formal and nonformal, worker and peasant education. Peasant education now concentrates on basic education (literacy eradication), agrotechnical training, and health, nutrition and family planning.

79. Literacy Eradication. In discussing peasant education it is necessary to begin with China's efforts to eradicate illiteracy. As noted earlier, even during the "1,000 character Pu ji method" of the 1920s Mass Education Movement and the "winter schools" of the Yenan days, the eradication of illiteracy among the masses was a priority. Despite sporadic attempts to promote literacy throughout the revolutionary struggle for independence in "liberated areas," the illiteracy rate was still hovering near 80 percent. With the founding of the People's Republic of China, Mao proclaimed that, "the eradication of illiteracy is a necessary condition for the construction of a new China." Following this proclamation, the First National Conference on Worker-Peasant Education in 1950 declared that "the basic task in worker-peasant education at present is to develop a literacy movement, gradually eliminating illiteracy." The goals at that time were to wipe out illiteracy among government cadre in two to three years, reach 90% literacy among workers in three to five years, and achieve nearly 70 percent literacy among peasants in seven years. The age group target of this literacy movement was those between the ages of 14 and 50. The major approach was a series of literacy campaigns throughout the country (Yao, 1980).

80. At this time, the criteria and measures for literacy were defined and remain in effect today. They are: (a) 1,500 character mastery for peasants and 2,000 for workers; (b) capacity to read the newspaper; (c) ability to write simple letters and fill in applications and other forms; and (d) passage of a simple test locally constructed to measure the above (a-c)

performance skills. In comparison to formal schooling, it is noteworthy that 3,000 characters mastery is considered to be a minimal level for primary school graduates (six years).

81. The initial campaigns to eradicate illiteracy followed a definite pattern. Typical principles of this pattern were provided by the directorate of the literacy program in Chonghua County: "(a) strengthen the administrative structure and form the teaching team; (b) grasp typical cases to arouse the masses; (c) determine teaching methods in the light of actual conditions; and (d) consolidate and develop the achievements."

82. In practice, literacy campaigns began with a period of planning and popularization, which usually entailed an "investigation" or survey of the literacy conditions in a given environment. In Xiang Fu People's Commune, for example, each illiterate had to make a plan indicating his/her own starting point for learning, an assessment of the learning conditions, how he/she would learn, and when he/she would carry the plan out. All plans had to be posted for public review, peer pressure could then be applied to ensure that the illiterate followed through with the plan. (For a complete list of literacy documents produced in Taojing Country alone during this early era, see Appendix G.)

83. This investigation stage was followed by "popularization" or raising the awareness of the need for literacy among the illiterates. Mass organizations such as the Communist Youth League had a special responsibility for the popularizing and mobilizing stages of the literacy effort. Model or pilot efforts were then launched, which were later extended and replicated in a given locality as they proved successful.

84. The final phase was a period of stabilizing and consolidating the program and creating a literacy environment by provisioning work-units with newspapers and libraries. "Step-by-step" was the basic motto adhered to during this period.

85. The gradual institutionalization of literacy efforts from anti-illiteracy classes (1954) through anti-illiteracy associations (1956) to the establishment of an anti-illiteracy headquarters (1958) and finally to the Committee for Worker-Peasant Education and County Division of Worker Peasant Education (1972) in Conguhua County, Guangdong Province is illustrative of the key role of the literacy drive in the evolution of the overall institutional development of the on-going Provincial and National Structure for worker-peasant education.

86. Teachers for the literacy efforts were drawn from students ("little teachers") and normal school teachers. During the "rustification" campaign of the Cultural Revolution, intellectuals and students were sent to the countryside to learn from the peasantry. Most of them were involved in promoting literacy as well. Unlike the voluntary efforts of students and

intellectuals in the anti-literacy drive of the pre-Cultural Revolution period, the "back to the countryside" program had compulsory and ideological bent. The "social laboratory" concept of James Yen during the 1920-1930s Mass Education Movement may have established the precedent for rustication efforts. At that time, students and intellectuals in Beijing voluntarily left the comforts of their "bourgeois" urban life style and headed to the neighboring rural area of Ting Hsien (Buck, 1968).

87. Often, literacy instructors were trained in the chain approach with the Provincial Division of Worker-Peasant Education providing training for County staff three times per year for three days, the County level training the Commune staff for twelve times per year for three days, the Commune staff in turn training the Brigade staff a half day per week throughout the program of literacy irradication.

88. Guided by the Party's Central Committee policy of "unfolding the campaign to read and write and reducing illiteracy step by step," teaching took place in homes, courtyards, and schools as "relatives taught relatives, neighbors taught neighbors, and children taught parents." Depending on the local conditions, instruction ranged from small group classes to one-on-one and self study. As stated by the Xiang Fu People's Commune Director, "In our work, we always pay attention to proceeding from actual conditions, different methods are adopted in accordance with different students, conditions, and desires. In order to give service to production, we insist that learning culture be integrated with learning technology, and class teaching with field practice." When the numbers were great, the collective or group approach dominated, as they shrunk more one-on-one and self-study evolved. Groups were frequently organized according to occupation and functional interest. Materials were locally produced with functional relevance. National literacy materials were also used to complement locally produced instructional materials. Study was scheduled in accordance with the seasonal work cycle. "Study more during the slack season, less during the busy season" took its place among the themes and mottos popularizing the campaign goals and methods.

89. Motivation to continue through the 200 hours of classroom instruction estimated for a person to become functionally literate was sustained by applying peer pressure; integrating economically useful knowledge, e.g., record keeping and agricultural information, into instructional materials; and combining literacy with cultural and life activities in general, e.g., entertainment and social activities (reading sessions). In some instances, it has been said that those refusing to attend classes were fined. Generally speaking, in a society in which jobs are assigned, it is relatively easier to make literacy standards a direct motivational tool by linking them to employment opportunities.

90. "Labeling" or affixing large characters to objects throughout homes and communities, was an important learning technique. As recounted in Jintang County, "A trainee named We Tai-Kun wrote names on the kitchen stove,

the water vat, the bed, the wardrobe, the cupboard etc., so that she could see these characters and memorize them more easily." This labelilng strategy also helped reinforce a person's motivation to take part in the literacy effort by making it more concrete.

91. All in all, the basic approach to motivation in China has been ideological and group-oriented, rather than material and individual-based. However, to motivate participation in literacy efforts, often teachers were rewarded with pens, notebooks, towels, mugs, and general accolades for producing new literates under the each-one-teach-one scheme.

92. Today the maintenance of a viable literacy environment is enhanced by the Government policy of insuring that 60 percent of books produced are allocated to rural areas. The "private picture book store" is a commonplace contemporary phenomenon throughout the Chinese urban and commune landscape. Here, a person can rent a book (usually short paperbacks) to read on the spot for the price of 3 fen (US$ 2 cents).

93. It is difficult to establish the exact cost of moving a person from a state of illiteracy to that of literacy (by Chinese standards). For example, in Chengdu District, Sichuan Province, we were told that it requires 23-28 yuan (US$15-18) to make a person literate. The exact breakdown of expenditure for this process was not provided, but one can assume that the major costs were for teachers' salaries and instructional materials. It was stated that the local government usually provides about 3 yuan (US$2) per person in grants and that the remainder of the cost was paid by the individual and or the commune through labor exchange.

94. While dropout rates were not normally available, in Chengdu District, the dropout rate of literacy classes was about 30 percent. This dropout rate is mostly attributed to competing opportunity costs of labor for agriculture.

95. For the 17-year period prior to the "Great Proletarian Cultural Revolution," the Chinese made substantial gains in eradicating illiteracy. During this period more than 100 million illiterates were freed from the bondage of ignorance, and literacy levels of numerous others were raised. However, the study team was told that with the ten years of chaos and turmoil which characterized the Cultural Revolution, systematic literacy efforts ground to a halt. The result was that many new literates lapsed back into illiteracy and a generation of youth remained unschooled and illiterate. In 1977, the literacy movement was resumed. Teachers and students were mobilized in a campaign approach reminiscent of past revolutionary days. For example, in Conghua County before liberation there was an illiteracy rate of 72.5 percent. From 1950 onward, winter schools and village schools were established throughout the countryside and, by 1955, many winter schools were turned into regular evening schools for peasants. After 1958, educational conditions improved and sparetime secondary schools teaching politics, culture, and technology sprang up. By

the advent of the Cultural Revolution illiteracy was reduced to 20 percent. Illiteracy in the county is presently down to three percent and the brigades now focus their attention on offering courses at primary and secondary school levels as well as upgrading agricultural technology.

96. Despite the success of Chonghua County's experience with illiteracy eradication, the national literacy level is currently estimated to be about 65 percent (World Bank, 1981). This means that there are over 100 million illiterate or semi-illiterate adults in China today. Rather than relying solely on the strategies of the mass campaign approach, the Chinese are now taking a cue from the health sector's comprehensive approach, which is "prevention first, cure second." Thus illiteracy is both prevented and attacked, and the general education of the people is improved by placing a clear emphasis on linking adult illiteracy eradication to universal primary schooling. Primary schools are now being encouraged to conduct sparetime literacy classes or to offer coursework based on the curriculum of the upper primary school to adults in the evenings.

97. Agrotechnical Training. The evolution of the commune structure into subordinate units of the production brigade and production team (roughly equivalent to the western geo-political divisions of county, town, and village, respectively) stems from the progressive collectivization of agriculture and dates back to the land reform of 1950. At that time the Government encouraged mutual aid teams (which likely emanated from existing traditional peasant modes of labor exchange) to become agricultural cooperatives in which peasants pooled their land and major means of production to obtain shares in the new cooperatives. In the mid-1950s, these cooperatives became "advanced cooperatives" and co-op members shared labor and land according to the principle of "from each according to his ability, to each according to his work." In 1958, when these latter units were viewed as too small in scale and too limited in manpower and funds, they were organized into larger units or communes under the auspices of the Central Committee's resolution to establish Peoples' Communes in the rural areas (Chou, 1975). Today, within such communes the propagation of private plots/8 is increasing and the collective agricultural system itself is undergoing considerable rethinking as the unit of accountability in some communes in certain areas has recently become the family and not the production team *per se*.

/8 Private plots have been growing at such a rate that some attribute erosion problem to the expansion of these plots in the worsening non-collectivized hills and up the mountain tops which surround the communes. As Printz and Steinle (1977) observed in their study of commune life in China, "Although the original percentage of private land (five percent) allocated since communalization was unchanged, the amount of land available for family plots had increased. The population had grown and more land had become available for cultivation thanks to continuing efforts to reclaim the mountain terrain for farming."

98. The change in the social-production relations in agriculture provide a structural framework for understanding the previously outlined organization and financing of current peasant training, or adult education, as related to the transmission of agricultural information and skills.

99. The principal adult education training unit in most rural areas is the sparetime agrotechnical middle school. This training unit is typically located in, and administered at, the commune level. It is an upper secondary-level school equivalency program which places its main emphasis on agriculture. The criteria for entry into such a school as reported by one such school in Shujing Peoples' Commune, Taojiang County, Hunan, is as follows: The candidate in agriculture training should: (a) play a critical role in managing production; (b) be at least a junior-middle school graduate; (c) be about 25 years old; (d) have set his mind on farm work and be interested in studying agricultural science; and (e) have some capability of organizing (Commune brief, 1981).

100. The primary subjects of these agrotechnical schools are: the cultivation of crops; the protection of plants; the use of soils and fertilizers; and the breeding of crops. The period of schooling is approximately two years. Each student who is selected to participate in such a program is released from production for 60 days fulltime study per year (6 hours a day, 4 days per month). Instruction focuses on solving urgent problems regarding farming during the busy cultivating season, and concentrates on imparting basic knowledge during the slack season. Thus, the students can apply the principles of scientific farming in their fields in a timely manner and increase their general educational background when their fields are idle.

101. Instructors for these programs are drawn from the technical staff of the Commune agromechanic workshop and agrotechnical station. They are compensated for their teaching time by the allocation of work points./10 Instructional materials are produced both locally or drawn from materials produced by the provincial and/or National Agriculture Departments. As in the area of worker education, the Bureau of Worker-Peasant Education is now attempting to introduce standardized curricula and competency exams. In addition to courses offered by standardized upper secondary level sparetime agrotechnical school, some agricultural courses are offered in the brigade-run sparetime junior secondary schools (which offer a middle secondary school equivalency program with the major subjects of instruction being mathematics, Chinese, and agri-sciences).

/10 Adult education teachers typically receive about 10-15 days in-service training at the commune or county level each year in the rural areas and at the teacher training (normal) colleges in the urban areas. To provide a feeling for teacher salary, in Sichuan Province urban teachers receive about 60 yuan (US$40) per month and rural teachers about 40 yuan (US$26) per month. Labor exchange and work points are also frequent forms of remuneration. However, as in the case of enterprises, teacher salaries vary in accordance with the overall income and priority investments of the Brigade/Commune production unit.

102. In addition to the sparetime schools at the commune and brigade levels, the commune agromechanic workshop and the commune agricultural station are said to offer periodic short courses to upgrade the skills of production brigade agrotechnical teams. These teams in turn meet with farmer groups during the slack season or with individuals in the field during the busy season to pass on new skills and knowledge, e.g., spacing of plants and fertilizer usage. The overall agricultural structure of research support and training at various levels within the commune and above to the provincial and national levels is roughly as follows:

KEY PEASANT AGRICULTURAL TRAINING INSTITUTIONS AND FUNCTIONS

Geo-Political Level	Key Training Institution	Major function
Nation	Ministry of Agriculture	Overall policy formulation
	Academy of Agricultural Sciences	Advanced training and research
	Wuhan Central China Agricultural College	
	Peking Agricultural College	
	Suzhou Agricultural College	Train lead agricultural Educators
Province	Agricultural universities and colleges	Train county level personnel
	Agricultural academies	Conduct research and supervise college research
Commune	Agrotechnical sparetime schools Agromechanical workshops Agrotechnical stations	Provide Preservice and inservice vice training for potential and existing production brigade agricultural teams. Schools offer upper secondary equivalency.
Production brigade/ team	Agrotechnical teams Sparetime middle schools	Train farmers Offer agricultural courses along with general junior secondary school equivalency

103. Results of agrotechnical sparetime education are usually reported in numbers of technical staff trained in agriculture for any given commune, rate of adoption/extension of new techniques, and changed levels of agricultural productivity. Though it is difficult to sort out confounding variables linking various interventions (including adult education) to changes in productivity, communes such as Luciduo Peoples' Commune in Taojiang County proclaim that "out of the 44 production teams where the graduates [sparetime agrotechnical schools] live and work, 40 increased their grain yield. Their output increase represented one-third of the output increase in the whole commune." According to extension performance criteria, they claim to have "popularized and extended" the following techniques through scientific experimental activities in 1980: (1) ridge and furrow cultivation of rice to an area of 930 mu, (2) saving of 210,000 jin of seeds due to less seed cultivation of rice, (3) success of late rice seeding and (4) ridge cultivation of sweet potatoes to 750 mu. In the absence of baseline data and comparative performance for similar communes, however, it is difficult to accept the Chinese proclamation of uncontested success.

104. Since the Study Team was primarily looking at adult education under the guidance and auspices of the Bureau for Worker-Peasant Education, attention was focused on the commune level sparetime agrotechnical secondary school and not on other agricultural training and research activities which are directly under the auspices of the Bureau of Agriculture (especially at the provincial and national levels). Therefore, financing can only be discussed in the context of these sparetime agrotechnical schools which are totally financed by the commune. For example, the costs quoted at Luciduo People's Commune were 30 yuan (US$20) per student for the two year program which lasted approximately 60 days (4 days per month and about six hours per day). The individual production brigades bore the cost of the students which they sent to the school. The teaching materials, administrative costs and school building were provided by the commune with some assistance from the State. This amounted to about 700 yuan (US$840) per year in Zhuyinda People's Commune. During their days of study the students are given work points by the commune and thus earn their usual income by converting their points. Board and book expenses are in effect born by their original units, and operational funds for staff salaries as well as capital facility costs (usually amounting to nothing as existing structures are used) come from the commune.

105. Two other innovative peasant agricultural adult education institutions of a historical nature, even though they are now nominally obsolete, are worth discussing. During the Cultural Revolution the so-called May 7 Peasant Agricultural Colleges functionally substituted for the present day

sparetime agrotechnical schools./11 In effect, the May 7 Peasant Agricultural College was an attempt to upgrade the status, if not the quality, of an agricultural secondary education to a college level, and to load it with ideological content so that it would serve as an instrument for breakingdown class distinctions and divisions between manual and intellectual worker and work. A parallel to this (sometimes integrated with the May 7 Peasant Agricultural College) was the decentralization of Agricultural College and University Faculties, which had formerly been centralized in and around major towns and cities. The intent was to locate individual faculties in communes throughout the country. This was not unlike the pattern of industrial extension of factory workshops discussed earlier. The Jiangsi Communist Labor University (Agricultural College) was one leading model for this program. It was reorganized in 1958, to train agricultural technicians and cadre (management) in the surrounding Jiangsi Province. At one point there were some 130 branch schools ("straw hut" universities) located in communes and production brigades throughout the countryside. The Chenyang Agricultural College in Liaoning Province was another example of this model. Dedicated to the principle that "crops could not be grown on black boards," research was done in situ on small farm plots with most instruction taking place in the field (Lucas, 1976). The Chao Yang Agricultural College, also an early model for the ruralization of higher education, was "held up as a model for the whole country and regarded as the educational equivalent of the Dazhai Brigade in agriculture" (Lofstede, 1980).

106. There is little empirical evidence to determine how well this latter innovation worked in terms of promoting relevant agricultural research and development. In fact, it is now the Government's intention to relocate and recentralize some of these faculties onto their original campuses.

107. In summarizing, the literacy and agricultural foci of adult education in the context of the rural commune today, the key institutions operating are: (a) upper primary and middle secondary sparetime schools under the administration and financing of brigades and production teams essentially for the purposes of providing basic education or raising the cultural level of peasants in a form, content, and level equivalent to the regular age-graded primary and junior secondary schools; (b) the commune run sparetime agricultural schools) providing sparetime upper secondary school equivalent agricultural based education primarily for lead peasants who are preparing to become production team agrotechnicians; (c) and short-course and field-based extension type training for peasant farmers offered by the brigade agrotechnical production teams and the staff of the commune agricultural research station and agromechanical workshops.

108. Other commune administered forms of adult education apart from basic school equivalency, literacy, and agricultural extension and training are sideline industry training through factory extension (already discussed

---

/11 Quoting from Shirk (1979), "According to Vice-Minister Pu, the May 7th Universities, the rural counterpart of the July 21st Universities, had never achieved true university levels of training and therefore are being downgraded to May 7th middle schools."

at length under worker education) and health, nutrition, and family planning education. A brief review of adult education activities for peasants in this latter category follows.

109. Health, Nutrition, and Family Planning Education. Herbalists, midwives, and acupuncturists who combine traditional and modern health care techniques exemplify the Chinese principle of "Walking on Two Legs," i.e., combining the old with the new. Most production brigades have a health unit staffed by about four workers selected by the brigade on the basis of past basic medical experience (traditional or modern) and general interest. This unit is the basic primary health care institution; outreach staff are known as "bare foot doctors."/12 Barefoot doctors receive at least one short training course in the basic principles of diagnosis, prescription, injection, midwifery and the preparation of herbal medicines. These short training courses are offered at the commune or country level by medical staff who have received training at provincial health centers.

110. The tasks of the local production brigade health unit, as noted during a visit to the "Red Cross Chapter" (Health Center) of Liangming Brigade, are as follows:

- to conduct training on first-aid and other health knowledge;
- to organize its members to mobilize people in joining the patriotic health campaign;
- to promote propaganda on health knowledge, thus raising the people's health-consciousness level;
- to coordinate with related departments on family planning propaganda and birth control guidance;
- to assist in propaganda and organizational work of blood donation campaigns;
- to improve the reporting system of epidemic diseases and encourage the masses to report incidence of epidemic diseases; and
- to carry out emergency care and simple treatment of minor injuries and illnesses.

/12 It should be pointed out that a community health care system using paraprofessional lay health workers locally selected, trained, and supervised to (1) record births and deaths; (2) vaccinate against smallpox; (3) promote clean water; and (4) provide simple first aid, basically serving as the "advance guard of scientific medicine" at the village level backed up by subdistrict Health Stations and District Health Centers was first developed in China from 1931-35 under the Tinghsien Mass Education Movement (see Chien, "Development of Systematic Training in Rural Public Health", Annual Report, International Rural Reconstruction Movement, New York: 1935).

111. Since primary health care programs have been described in great detail elsewhere (e.g., Rogers and Chen, 1980), they will not be treated further here. However, like the worker and peasant education programs in industry, agriculture, and basic education, health training is currently being qualitatively upgraded with standardization and certification being an integral part of this process.

112. Family planning, child care, and nutrition education fall under the auspices of the Bureau of Health, the National Federation of Women (a mass organization), and more specifically, the "women's worker," an adult education role found in every commune. The major tasks of women's workers are to organize weekly meetings of women's groups to discuss women's issues and to disseminate child care, nutritional, and family planning information. The National Federation of Women is the mass organization which provides the backup support and training to these frontline women's cadre. Maternal and child care, children's education (particularly preschool), and the promotion of women's participation in productive and political activities are the major goals of the National Federation of Women which are implemented by the women's worker. Nutrition education generally takes a back seat to more visible preventative health care priorities, such as immunization, nor do nutritional considerations appear to be well-integrated in agricultural policies.

Local Government Sponsored Adult Education

113. Enterprise, commune, and production brigade sponsored adult education insitutions are all educational, productive, and political (governance) in nature. There is yet a third set of local governmental institutions which sponsor adult education activities. These are located predominantly in cities and large rural towns and are not directly engaged in production. An excellent example of this is the Honkow Avocational Institute, a district (local) government administered and financed adult education program in Honkow District, Shanghai Municipality. Actual costs were not available. The Institute offers six major areas of study: mechanical engineering and machine design and fabrication; electronic engineering and automation; chemical engineering for chemical analysis; environmental chemical analysis; Chinese literature; and foreign language. These are provided in a four year, two semester per year program of 20 weeks per semester. Approximately 17 instructional hours per week are usually offered in three half-day working hours and two sparetime evening sessions. Upon completing required course work and passing standardized exams, students are granted tertiary degrees equivalent to that of East China Normal University, an affiliated regular institution of higher learning.

114. Faculty are drawn from neighboring universities and the professional and technical staff of enterprises. There is a fulltime staff of 133 teachers and 85 "visiting" or part-time instructors. Costs are totally borne by the Honkow District Government. Instructional materials and

content are the same as those used by regular universities and colleges. There are 10 such district-run sparetime colleges in Shanghai and one major municipal run sparetime college. The arrangement is very similar to that of a North American state university and junior college system, but it is organized exclusively for workers pursuing degrees on a parttime and spare time basis, with release time and financial support from employers. Instruction takes place primarily through T.V., correspondence courses, and classroom lectures held in an old city building, formerly a District post office. Practical work is coordinated on-site in neighboring factory workshops. The Institute also offers sparetime secondary education courses but on a much smaller scale than the university equivalency program. The Institute has over 64 classes with a total enrollment of 2,572 students. The Institute began in 1958 with two areas of study, mechanical and chemical engineering, but was forced to close during the Cultural Revolution. It is now in a period of "reconstruction and rehabilitation" with plans to become "Hankow Adult Education Center" by 1982, and to offer a wider range of university and secondary school degree equivalency programs, as well as other short specialized courses.

115. A second example of a municipal/district administered adult education program is the Guangzhou Sparetime College founded in 1962, a comprehensive college for workers. The college has four major departments: mechanical, electrical, and chemical engineering, and Chinese language and literature. Courses in mathematics, foreign language, and political science are also offered.

116. There are four different programs: four year specialized university equivalency programs (8-13 hours per week); two-three year teacher training courses (9-14 hours per week); single subject courses for one to two or so years (3-5 hours per week); and six month special short courses (3-4 hours per week) in such areas as T.V. repair, literature and language study. In addition to these offerings, the college conducts special classes for industrial and commercial accountants under the auspices of the Municipal Bureau of Finance as well as courses for lawyers and judges through the Provincial Bureau of Justice.

117. As in the Honkow Institute, admission is by examination; textbooks are selected from those used by fulltime colleges and universities and supplemented by locally produced materials geared to meet special learner needs. There is a full-time staff of 165 teachers with an enrollment of about 4,022 students in over 47 classes. The college leadership estimates that the cost of training a qualified technical graduate is approximately 1,000 yuan (US$660) while that of educating a liberal arts student is about 7,000 yuan (US$400). It costs about 318 yuan (US$210) per student per semester at Honkow Institute. If students take an average of 17 class hours including lab work per week for a 20 week semester then the unit cost can be roughly estimated to be about 340 student class hours per

semester divided by 318 yuan (US$210) student semester or 1.1 yuan (US$.75) per student instructional hour.

118. The Director of the Institute estimates a two percent dropout/failure rate per annum. The failure/dropout rate at Shanghai Municipal Sparetime University was estimated to be one percent for full time students and 30-40 percent for short courses. The reasons given for the large number of short-course dropouts were work load, family problems, and job transfer. On another note, female enrollment at these two institutions was 25 percent and 10 percent, respectively. The argument was that not too many women were interested in the engineering field which was the major emphasis of these programs.

119. While many of these local government conducted adult education programs suffer from a shortage of up to date equipment and a lack of instructional facilities, some are admirably drawing strength from the regular state university system (books, faculty, curriculum) to meet the growing need for trained manpower and the demand for higher education and specialized training.

Mass Organizations and Adult Education

120. Mass organizations have served primarily mobilizational (organizational), motivational (popularizing) and instructional (communication) functions in the larger scheme of worker-peasant education in China. They have also, in varying degrees provided financing for adult education activities. The major mass organizations operating in China are: the All China Federation of Workers; the National Federation of Women; and the Communist Youth League./13

121. In general, mass organizations are the catalyzing agents of adult education. Adult education in China has been organized essentially along lines of functional interest groups, e.g., women, workers, farmers, and youth. The role of mass organizations as natural channels for organizing these functional groups of learners and creating learner demand through popularization and peer pressure is critical in the horizontal spread and vertical influence of adult education in China.

122. All China Federation of Workers. Prior to the Cultural Revolution (during which period many were blacklisted), labor unions not only made a substantial financial contribution to the adult education of workers but in many instances directly initiated and administered factory run sparetime colleges and secondary schools. Originating from the Government Adminis-

---

/13 The Chinese Communist Party and the People's Liberation Army, while important mass institutions for education and training, were not covered by the Study Team and will not be treated here. Although it can be said that the Party has enormous direct and indirect influence over the mass organizations which are discussed in this paper.

trative Council's "Directives on Developing Sparetime Education for Workers and Staff Members" of June 1950, trade unions were given the task of mobilizing for the implementation of sparetime worker education.

123. Unions also conducted cadre or leadership training for union leaders. Initially, such courses included mobilization and organizational techniques, ideology, and literacy. As summarized by Harper (1964), "although no systematic technical education program was instituted [at that time], master-apprentice contracts and occasional lectures and campaigns were used to promote advanced techniques at the Wusan factory." By 1956, complete factory-based sparetime technical education programs, which placed emphasis on technical rather than political training, had evolved. However, due to the thrust to increase productivity of the Great Leap Forward, time for study decreased, the number of qualified teachers dwindled and a general lack of qualified students and funds all converged to make production and study mutually exclusive. Only in the period between the Great Leap Forward and the Cultural Revolution (1961-65) did a more comprehensive and realistic system of worker education which stressed different levels of worker aptitude and offered a variety of sparetime schools, e.g. upper primary, junior secondary, etc., to meet individual worker needs - begin to exist. Unfortunately, during the Cultural Revolution the "revisionist" label took its toll on the labor education movement, and it is just now beginning to restore its pre-Cultural Revolution momentum and once again play a key role in adult-worker education.

124. An exceptional example of a sparetime college run by the trade unions is that recently reported in the Beijing Review (1981) run by the Beijing Municipal Council of Trade Unions. It enrolls 885 students selected by examination from 3,580 candidates in the main subject areas of electrical engineering, Chinese, mathematics, industrial accounting, statistics, and environmental protection. Classes are held three half days and two evenings per week and students are released at full pay and benefits from their respective enterprises to attend classes.

125. Workers' Palaces were also established in a number of cities providing both recreational, library, and educational programs. In a recent visit to the Shanghai Workers' Palace, a trade union sponsored recreational cum educational facility, the Director of the Palace stated that the Palace was a "college for the workers - in a sense a place of learning as well as a paradise with the primary goals of serving the workers and the Socialist Revolution." In line with the three principles of labor education - to raise political consciousness, to enrich general knowledge, and to entertain variety in life - activities at the Palace range from public lectures to singing-dancing competitions. There were several study areas and a large library-reading room as well as a general game area. The Palace is now conducting 32 formal courses with an enrollment of over 6,000 workers. These are typically short courses to raise basic educational levels and to improve the quality of job related worker performance. Courses are also offered in specialized areas such as foreign language and energy conservation. The staff try to relate all courses to the needs of the workers and

practical problem solving. Exams devised by the Palace are used to select students for participation in the heavily subscribed courses. An example was given where only 250 of 500 applicants were admitted to a business management course via exam criterion. Student records are kept and communicated to factories. Union and Palace staff keep in close contact with factory education committees to assess what workers need, what they have already learned, and the like. There are only three permanent educational staff so the Palace must rely on outside visiting faculty from regular schools and factory professionals and technicians to teach their courses. Teachers are motivating and training others to be teachers. As the Palace Director stated, "We light a candle here and put light in the whole room."

126. The present All China Federation of Workers, as labor unions go, is somewhat different than the North American-Western European union in terms of the priority which is placed on various activities. Chinese unions are more concerned with worker education, more specifically political education under the party directives, than with traditional labor-management wage-benefit negotiations. As Harper (1964) notes "the trade union cadre must endeavor to bridge the gap between the interests of the workers and those of the State; to do this he must succeed in transmitting the ideology of the Party to the working masses."

127. In theory, the workers are the State and the union is the management in China, thus the mobilization of workers _for_ the State rather than in protest _against_ the State is the current _modus operandi_. The current lower union political profile may indeed be a result of the aftermath of the Cultural Revolutionary period; unions appear to be reverting to their late 1950s and early 1960s focus on technical rather than political education of workers, while the Party is contriving to maintain indirect influence and control over workers' education as administered and implemented by the union cadre. In 1978, at the Tenth National Congress of Chinese Trade Unions the basic objectives of the unions were stated: "to unite, educate and help the workers and staff members steadily to raise their political consciousness, acquire scientific knowledge and technological skill, take an active part in enterprise management, launch socialist labor emulation drives, raise labor productivity, gradually improve the material and cultural life of the worker and staff members on the basis of increased production, and strive towards building a powerful, modernized, socialist China as early as possible" (Pao, 1980). The eleven years hiatus in the All China Federation of Trade Unions activities had finally come to an end.

128. After quoting Lenin, "The trade union is a Communist university," one union official the Hunan Provincial Symposium on Adult Education (fieldnotes, 1981) proceeded to say that, "the unions would now take the lead in worker education again, by: mobilizing the masses to understand the importance of adult education, implementing an organization and leadership in all departments and enterprises with full time cadre in charge of adult

education, conducting a general survey of worker cultural and technological levels in order to modify adult education programs based on factual analysis of learner levels and requirements, and to implement methods of providing trained teachers for adult education."

129. National Federation of Women. In theory, the main function of this mass organization is to defend the benefits and rights of women in politics, economics (work), and social life. As spelled out in the Fourth National Women's Congress in 1978, the tasks of women's organizations are: "to support, encourage and organize women in their effort to study politics, enhance their literacy, study science and technology and the skill of management, so as to raise their ideological, educational and technical levels; to propagate and implement the principle of equality between men and women and the policy of equal pay for equal work and to protect the rights and interests of women and children; to cooperate with relevant departments in promoting collective welfare and social service for women and children; and to improve the work concerning their health and family planning" (Pao, 1980).

130. Women's groups exist at all levels of government down to the brigade production team. At the commune level, there is a Women's Committee with a representative of that Committee on the Commune General Committee for Worker-Peasant Education. Women's committees also exist at the Provincial and National levels. At the Commune brigade level there is a Women's Worker, whose role and function were described under peasant education. At the production team level, are organized women's groups. Additionally, women play roles as mass teachers in evening literacy classes (sparetime primary and secondary schools), facilitators for women's groups, and the like.

131. Organizing women to study and learn has been the major activity of the National Federation of Women since its founding in 1949. The promotion of scientific agriculture and industrial skills, birth planning, and spare-time basic education are the main adult education content areas for women's groups. Child care is also an important topic of study. This includes the inculcation of collective values to counter the "only child (spoiled individual) syndrome" caused by the growing number of one-child families.

132. Health education for prospective mothers is another focal area of women's education. Courses cover pre-natal to post-natal periods of maternal care and child development. Short training courses are organized for a range of infant and child caregivers - employed sitters, infant nursery staff, grandparents, and other family members. The Women's Worker, with the support of the Federation (and in cooperation with the Bureau of Health), is responsible for parent education. The Central Committee has recently assigned the National Federation of Women the task of coordinating all agencies for children's education from the performing arts, traditionally under the Bureau of Culture, to children's literature produced by the Bureau of Education.

133. While marriage, inheritance, and employment laws have at least in legal and rhetorical terms improved the status of women in China, female participation rates in work and adult educational activities are still below their proportional representation in society at the large. Although the Chinese have come a long way in the last thirty plus years in promoting the equal opportunity and welfare of women primarily through the efforts of adult education, they would be the first to admit that there is still a long way to go. As the now infamous Jiang Chiang once observed in an interview with Roxane Witke, "ideals and reality should not be confused; women still have a long way to go in China. Custom died hard in rural areas. Arranged marriages, celebrations and costly feasts could not be endured in a Socialist State. Despite agrarian reforms, women still allowed themselves to be given smaller or inferior parcels of land" (Mitgang, 1977).

134. The Communist Youth League (CYL). The Communist Youth League, Young Pioneers, student and other youth associations have always been both objects and instruments of adult education and political change in China. Today, the CYL has over fifty million members and is entrusted by the Party with guiding the Young Pioneers, China's mass organization of about 170 million children. The League also has the task of mobilizing and motivating young workers (under 28) as stated in a recent Xinhua (1980) editorial, "the Plant Youth League Committee attaches importance to political and ideological work among young workers and gives particular attention to helping those lagging behind."

135. As Young Pioneers during the early revolutionary period and as Red Guards during the Cultural Revolution, Chinese youth have historically been involved as learners and teachers in adult education. Chinese officials now openly share their concerns over the crisis of confidence of the youth, who were deeply affected by the Cultural Revolution-Red Guard and rustification activities. The young people's confusion over conflicting values resulting from recent ideological shifts coupled with the problem of youth unemployment could be a critical watershed for the current Government leadership. The Government's concern about the psychological problems of its young people is so great that a major youth education campaign called the "Four Beauties" (mind, language, behavior, and environment) and "Five Talks" (health, social order, morality, civilization, and politeness) is now underway.

136. Children's palaces continue to exist "providing guided recreational and learning activities, carrying out a significant program of education extending far beyond the schoolroom" (Chen, 1978). In addition, Youth Palaces, whose central purpose is to reintegrate youth into main stream post-Maoist Chinese society through adult education are currently being stressed. The Shanghai Youth Palace, for example, is a recreational and education center providing a range of services from career and psychological counseling to public lectures and short courses to enhance basic education and teach marketable technical skills. Youth are also being organized into

professional "survival groups" to open up small street canteens and businesses in order to tackle the unemployment problem. Talks are organized to bring persons from varying age groups together in an effort to bridge the generation and ideological gaps. Such programs are usually financed by municipal and local governments.

137. While the rustification program has not been totally abandoned, it is no longer compulsory. Manual labor is still considered an important part of the educational experience for youth (Chen, 1978); however, many young people who were forcibly relocated in rural areas are now flocking to the cities in search of their future. Showing idealism that may not be the norm, one former youth who went "down to the villages and up to the mountains" and is presently a sparetime factory college student stated:

> We are very anxious about the future of our country. We could not see prospects for our generation because we lost the cream of our youth during the Cultural Revolution. Now the most important thing is to make up for our loss. Even though I am over thirty and married I still feel young and want to do something for my country. Many students in my class are mature and energetic and still think that they can do many things.

The challenge for adult education is to channel this feeling and energy into reintegrating Chinese youth into the work force and general life of the nation. The propagation of youth palaces and mass campaigns are steps in that direction.

The Mass Media

138. The final all pervasive adult education institution is the mass media. Using the electronic media of radio and T.V.; the printed media of correspondence materials, bulletin boards, chalkboards, posters, flyers, newspaper and libraries; museums and exhibitions; lectures and assemblies; and face-to-face communication, the Chinese are masters at providing a media blitz which rivals any commercial advertising campaign in the capitalist world. At the receiving end, one can typically find residential and workplace study groups organized by neighborhood, production team, and workshop education committees into informal listening and educational forums.

139. Access to and proliferation of the mass media, is considered an indicator of development. On a wall chart depicting commune success at the Xiang Fu Commune, the number of public address speakers was given along with more traditional indicators of development such as number of mu under cultivation and grain output. Parish and Whyte (1978) similarly noted that in the 45 villages they used as a data base, 39 had a broadcast network (see Appendix J for Basic Commune Data).

140. Television and Radio Broadcasting. Beijing Broadcasting-Television University was first set up in 1960 as an institution of higher learning on the air waves. It was supplemented by classroom tutoring and self-study via correspondence course materials. It was dissolved in 1969 in the midst of the Cultural Revolution and only recently resumed operation in 1979. Its national counterpart, the Central Broadcasting and Television University formed in February 1979, similarly offers a three-year college equivalency course which includes instruction in math, physics, chemistry, and English. The classes are aired nationwide in over 30 special T.V. universities which are locally administered by cities and provinces. The T.V. University is also plugged into numerous enterprises throughout the country with local stations in such major cities as Beijing, Shanghai, and Guangzhou offering specialized courses in teacher training, secondary school equivalency, and technical education. Nationwide about 420,000 students are registered on a parttime or fulltime basis in the National Central T.V. University (McCormick, 1980). Tuition is free and local enterprises or municipal government often purchase the ground equipment necessary for reception and organize and pay for tutorial services and textbooks. Students include workers, teachers, army personnel, and unemployed youth. Enrollment targets and costs are as follows:

TV UNIVERSITY: ENROLLMENT TARGETS, 1980-90

	1980	1985	1990
Total enrollments ('000) (full-time and part-time)	420	1,200	2,000
Number of year-long courses offered	18	50	100
Central Broadcasting and TV University (Beijing)			
(i) staff		700	2,000
(ii) space (sq m)		40,000	130,000
(iii) foreign exchange requirements ($ millions)	3.3	6.3	12.6
Total staff/a of central and provincial TV universities		10,000+	40,000

/a Estimated at one teaching staff member per 50 students and one administrative staff member per 100 students.
Source: Hultin, 1981.

To illustrate the range of students composition in a given urban area the following student enrollment breakdown was obtained from Beijing T.V. University for 1979:

ENROLLMENT BREAKDOWN
BEIJING T.V. UNIVERSITY (1979)

Occupation	Number of Students	Percentage
Workers	11,543	39.7
Government functionaries	3,472	12.0
Scientific and technical personnel	9,240	31.8
Teachers	3,411	11.8
People's Liberation Army	1,396	4.8

Note: The total 1979 cohort is 29,062 students.

141. Since the early days of T.V. and radio broadcasting, the curriculum has markedly expanded to include a broad range of university topics and areas of study from electronics to computer science and language. Texts are those used by regular degree-granting institutions of higher learning and supplemental materials are produced by the local sponsoring units, e.g., factories, municipalities. There are regular homework assignments, examinations, and certificates as in any normal degree granting formal educational program (Zhenhua, 1980). Students typically spend about four hours a week viewing and eight hour per week doing homework.

142. It actually costs the T.V. university about 20 yuan (US$24) per student per semester. Employers typically pay for setting up classes, tutors' salaries, and lab experiments. Unemployed youth attending classes usually pay a small fee to cover their costs, but local governments (municipal and district) often provide most of what is required to conduct the courses. Such district government-sponsored sparetime educational institutions are oriented toward T.V. University students who are unemployed and provide references to prospective employers of their graduates.

143. As in other educational programs, scant systematic tracer data on graduates is presently available, but based on student achievement, all indications are that the T.V. instruction program is a heralded success. For example at Guangdong Radio and T.V. University, Foshan Branch, after two years study 96.2 percent of those students (600) taking electronics and mechanical engineering courses reportedly passed the 1979 national examinations. For Beijing Branch T.V. and Radio University, the pass ratio of third term students (7,941) who were enrolled on the average in over four subjects, was 86.5 percent.

144. While the T.V. University has been criticized for not attempting to use teaching techniques which might be better suited to the medium (at present, most courses are presented in lecture form); being understaffed, not having adequate printed or other instructional materials, e.g., kits for

science as used in the British Open University, and having a very poor technical quality and low capacity, the ambitious efforts which have been made by this relatively young national educational venture are noteworthy (see Appendix I). Although still concentrated in urban areas, with T.V. ownership growing (from 630,000 in 1977 to over seven million sets today) due to increased output and reduced costs, T.V. is an educational medium to be reckoned with in China's future adult education plans.

145. Printed Media. Enough cannot be said about China's use of printed media. Daily newspapers are publicly posted in communes, factories, and neighborhoods; mini-novels are available for rent through the private picture book network; billboarads, charts, posters, and character sketches abound. The public eye is continuously being selectively exposed, informed, and guided. However, when examining libraries, Study Team Media Specialist, H. Campbell (1981) observed: "In factory, commune and public libraries, the methods are largely those of closed access to material, severe penalties for infraction of rules, occasional need to surrender identify cards to secure materials to read and much control of access in general. This results in a proportional low use of the facilities which, although numerous and generally isolated, have a high percentage of out-of-date material, and do not provide an integrated service to the uses."

146. Folk Media. Traditional media, social drama, and face-to-face communication were essential development communication apparatus of the Mass Education Movement/14 as well of the propaganda teams that were formed during the early revolutionary years. During the Cultural Revolution, revolutionary opera, social drama, dance and song troupes mixed socialist politics with art and mass communications. Based on Mao's Yenan Art Forum talk, the arts became politicized and proletarianized to serve the masses in their quest for a Socialist State. Most of the same folk communication media are now being filled with the re-emergence of neo-Confuscian Chinese cultural themes (Howard, 1978). In instances where such media are now serving development goals, it is generally in relationship to the popularization of science, technology, and the "four modernizations."

147. While the debate continues as to whether art and literature should be for life's sake or mere tools of socialist politics, a balance between these conflicting views is now surfacing. This was best expressed in a recent editorial quoting the late Mao Dun, Minister of Culture (1949-65) deposed during the Cultural Revolution:

/14 As Yen (1934) acclaimed, "Literature, drama, painting, the great historical characters of Chinese history, and the modern medium of radio are to be marshalled for intellectual and spiritual nourishment of the people as well as for their recreation, to create a reconstruction mentality, and ultimately, to rediscover the soul of the race and revitalize it for the modern world."

> Literature cannot be reduced to diagrams of political movements but the artist must arm himself with dialetical and historical materialism if he hopes to capture the essence, the main trend and the direction of things in the great complexity of real life.

148. The role of mass media can be summarized as follows: to propagate government plans and policies, to exchange experiences (inform and educate), to praise model efforts such as good teachers and productive enterprises, to criticize bad experience and laggards, and to entertain. It has always had this role though content has changed to reflect the ideological and development themes of the times. As Walls (1980) so aptly summarized, "The ruling establishment in China always recognized the power of the popular media to influence behavior by providing dramatic examples of good and evil, reward and punishment, success and failure".

Issues and Lessons from the Chinese Experience

149. Despite the periods of political turmoil and unrest and the radical shifts between ideological/educational foci which have characterized China's recent history, the results of its efforts at worker-peasant education over the past thirty years (1950-80) have been most impressive in absolute, if not, relative terms. It is reported that from 1978-81 alone over 130 million new literates have been generated and over 38 million semi-literates have been raised to primary school equivalency level. An additional 3.3 million workers and peasants have obtained secondary school equivalency and 200,000 have reached the level of higher education equivalency through adult education programs. About 80 percent of the participants of worker-peasant education programs have been promoted to ranks of technician, engineer, or other leading positions and now form the "backbone" of China's development (Yao, 1981). About one-half million workers are currently enrolled in factory-run universities and in sparetime colleges sponsored by provinces and municipalities. In addition, there are approximately 30 million students in sparetime schools run by enterprises, communes, production brigades, workers' and youth palaces, local government, regular universities, among other institutions (see Annex L).

150. There is little doubt that, from the Chinese viewpoint, the most important functions of adult education have been political socialization (value change), the solving of practical problems in industry and agriculture, and the raising of the basic educational (cultural) level of the masses. Relative priority on these three aspects of adult education has shifted over the past three decades as ideological forces have struggled for, and exchanged, power, but all three aspects have always been evident.

151. Currently the priority of adult education efforts is placed on worker and cadre (leadership-management) training in support of achieving the goals of the "Four Modernizations." As one plant director of sparetime education stated: "Most students are from factories and have over 10 years experience, so their goals are clear. Apart from theory, they wish to bring up their ability to deal with practical problems they encounter in their daily work." Commenting on the recent National Conference on Adult Education Mr. Heng Wei, Director Bureau of Education, Shanghai Municipality and Deputy

Director of the National Committee of Worker-Peasant Education, told the Study Team that the Central Committee recently submitted a document on adult education which outlines the priority tasks:

> We shall formalize adult education step by step, the preliminary concept is to achieve a systematic and preliminary formalized adult education system. The first task is to enlighten leaders of all enterprises to the fact that adult education is closely related to productivity. In order to increase productivity we must go for adult education. We must coordinate short term and long term planning. We must organize national coordinating committees in each province, city, county, and commune to coordinate work and to plan adult education across bureaus of varying ministries.

He further added that increasing financing, upgrading teaching, generating student places, and improving instructional materials would be the operational targets. Of course, one is quick to question the meaning and wisdom of such steps to formalize adult education given the general worldwide view that a major strength of adult nonformal education programs is its ability to be flexible and react to changing and diverse learner needs due to the absence of a constraining formalized structure.

152. This is not to say that peasant education or basic education is being ignored, but only to note that it is presently a lesser priority - one which is being handled in local contexts, e.g., communes and production brigade, and linked to other training or educational activities, e.g., primary schools offering sparetime primary school equivalency (basic literacy studies) in the evening and factories offering sparetime secondary school equivalency to prepare workers for further training in technical and professional sparetime programs. "Do in accordance with local conditions" is the underlying principle of present-day peasant education program offerings.

153. While adult education is applied and production linked wherever possible, it is currently being pursued as an equivalent to formal education in quality, certification, social status, and financial remuneration. It supplements and builds upon any previous formal education of participants. Hawkins (1979) accurately summarizes this tendency toward equivalency and institutionization: "the message here seems to be that these kinds of programs (alternative adult education) are allowable provided students reach comparable levels with students in the more conventional formal colleges and universities."

154. The above outlined parameters set for adult education in turn guide the design of adult education programs. They: (1) must focus on quality, not only on quantity; (2) must have an immediate application and an identifiable economic payoff, and, therefore, must directly relate to increasing unit production; and (3) should be in accordance with concrete conditions, and thus, meet identified local needs. The Government is now attempting to develop a more systematic and institutionalized adult

education network with committees for worker-peasant education at all levels of the political hierarchy from the national to the communal level. This measure will be supplemented by the design of caurses to upgrade the leadership skills of cadre and instructors and by the coordination of instructional materials development. A series of national and provincial materials development conferences at which guiding principles for instructional materials and actual texts, worksheets, and activities in accordance with these principles are produced are now underway. Research activities to assess learning needs, identify appropriate teaching methods and strategies, compile syllabi, and generally review the experience in worker-peasant education over the past thirty years are now being planned as tasks of adult education committees at the provincial level.

155. The persistent questioning of the Study Team by Chinese educators on topics regarding research and evaluation techniques may provide evidence that the Chinese are now seeking pragmatic solutions to problems which emerged during their past efforts at providing comprehensive adult education, and that they will subsequently make "substantive compromises with the Cultural Revolution education system" (Pepper, 1980).

156. The Chinese clearly view the current era of adult education and development as a period of restoring, restructuring, and consolidating the better elements of earlier programs, particularly those of the 1950-1958 and 1961-1965 periods. Consequently, the fear that the baby may be thrown out with the bath water regarding the abandonment of adult education innovations introduced during the Great Leap Forward and Cultural Revolution periods may be premature. For example, recently attempts to discredit Harbin Workers' Sparetime University were thwarted when its sparetime college graduates were tested and scored on a par with the graduates of regular universities who had pursued similar industrial architectural curricula. Also Jiangxi Communist Labor University has recently been held up as a model for sparetime colleges because of its effectiveness in offering short term training and correspondence courses and in using traveling teachers (Hawkins, 1979; also Kobayashi and King, 1980).

157. Presently, the educational pendulum is swinging toward the institutionalization of an adult education program which emphasizes quality and legitimacy over equality and access. Historically the first five-year plan stressed production linked with training; the Great Leap Forward's pendulum swung toward production linked to ideology; the Post Leap marked a return to the production-training nexus; and the Cultural Revolution's swing reinstated the supremacy of ideology over training. Today training is linked to production and certification; politically speaking, industrial and economic readjustment has led to educational readjustment. "Learn from Tachai [a successful agricultural commune]," "Model Jiangxi Labor University," among other such quotes, are visibly being replaced throughout the countryside on schools, houses, and factory walls by others more akin to the "Four Modernizations".

158. It was stated in several discussions with the Study Team that technological and organizational adjustments in enterprises and agriculture logically allow workers and peasants more time to participate in adult education programs. Parenthetically such education programs also serve a caretaker function for potentially under- and unemployed workers. However, this still begs the question of whether or not certification will open up more employment opportunities for the hordes of rural youth now immigrating, often illegally, to the cities. This group includes about 20 million youth who because of the upheavals of the cultural revolution still require cultural and technological upgrading to the middle school level.

159. In many areas, changing conditions have meant changing demands. For example, in the area of health, the requirements of primary health care staff have been reached and the focus has now shifted to upgrading the skills of those currently serving as barefoot doctors and to screening out those who cannot meet the newly-set, higher standards of performance. Chinese peasants now demand better quality health care (as a direct outcome of having had their basic health needs met). Will it be possible for the barefoot doctor system to provide access to health care of higher quality? What will happen to those barefoot doctors who don't make the grade? Also, the current stress on worker education may be potentially detrimental to farmers (who still comprise the majority of the population) in terms of access and equity. Down-playing peasant education could in the long run increase inequality and alienate the masses since the "trickle-down" distance is much greater in a resource tight environment with mass demands, such as China has, than elsewhere. On the other hand, one could also speculate that increasing peasant education opportunity could also fuel rising frustrations due to higher employment expectations which are unequalled by a slower growth in actual job opportunities.

160. What are some of the major lessons one might draw from the Chinese experience in adult education to date? First and foremost is that the mobilization of a political will, the creation of a strong bureaucratic organization, and the establishment of a definitive planning process which endeavors to coordinate demands with available delivery services are *sine qua non* of China's adult education success. The Chinese educational bureaucracy not only penetrates vertically to the lowest level through the Party, the Army, and the Government cadre - but it also spreads horizontally - through key mass organizations such as the Communist Youth League, All China Federation of Workers, National Federation of Women, and mass media. It is a broadly based and participatory organizational mode which serves the double function of promoting communication and of standing ready to serve as a mechanism for exercising political social control. As Lin (1975) succinctly stated "putting planning and coordination back in the hands of local authorities has the effect of enhancing self-reliance within the overall framework of national planning."

161. This uniquely Chinese strategy of extending adult education both vertically and horizontally provides for decentralized planning, local finance, control, and commitment - including responsibility and accountability - and insures that adult education offering will meet the needs of the lowest societal levels, e.g., production teams, neighborhood committees, workshop units. On the other hand, central authorities at every political level, guide, influence, and sanction the planning, policy setting, and decision making of the entire development process. Upper-level units require that all units - from production teams to health centers and factory workshops submit plans for the provision of adult education plans; and even study plans from individual adult learners. As stated by one Jintang county official, "The plan should be concrete to every person to be trained and open to all so that it can be carried out without failure under the supervision of the masses."

162. A second key lesson lies the Chinese use of "modeling," "meetings," "on spot conferences," and other ad hoc group arrangements in a decentralized but controlled system for promoting the exchange of experiences and the summing up of lessons. China has a built-in organizational learning capacity by continuously encouraging the sharing of experiences and the critical analysis of how the lessons of a given experience might be applied in varying conditions. Such a systematic means for applying new and old knowledge in various settings makes China look like one large "learning exchange." Rogers and Chen (1980) refer to this process as summarized in the Chinese slogan, "Grasp both ends and move the middle forward," meaning the most advanced units should provide models for others on a widespread basis, as a means of "horizontal diffusion."

163. A third important lesson lies in the Chinese ability to mobilize unused and under-utilized material and human resources, integrating the two to make for a balanced or eco-system approach to development. Factory and school staffs and facilities provide educational services to both adults and youth. Traditional herbalists become front-line health care workers. Those who have lost their jobs due to the introduction of mechanized agriculture are often gradually integrated into a commune's developing sideline agro-industry. One might say that the Chinese see the forest as well as the trees in every development endeavor.

164. A fourth lesson concerns the realm of motivation. "Popularization" is a key Chinese educational concept. User demand regarding government policy and the functional use of ensuing adult education programs is created through "pre-education" or "consciousness-raising." For example, during the literacy campaigns, propaganda teams were sent to communes to publicize relevant documents and instructions of the State Council among the peasants. Peer pressure, exercised through the praising of models and the criticism of failures by the mass media and mass organizations, is instrumental in further motivating potential users to the advantage of available programs. Wall posters, billboards, chalkboards, public meetings, among other media, are

highly visible methods of reward and sanction in China. It was stated that in one region of the country the "preparation of the soil" for the literacy program through popularization preceded the actual classes by over one year.

165. China's models of educational extension may provide a fifth lesson. Their three extension models - (a) program extension, exemplified by factory workshop extension to build sideline industries in the countryside and street industries in the urban neighborhoods; (b) the institutional extension model, for example, moving agricultural college faculties from urban environs to the rural communes; and (c) the information extension model, as demonstrated by the mass campaign approach for health, literacy, and family planning - all have many elements which could be replicated in other development settings. However, according to Study Team findings, the Chinese are now downplaying these innovative extension models. For example, sideline industries are being shut down or consolidated into larger production units (in order to reach economies of scale); agricultural college faculties are being reconcentrated into their original urban centers; and campaigns for literacy, health, etc., are now being relegated to institutional primary school and health center-based models of delivery. It is questionable as to whether or not innovative programs of previous eras have been adequately evaluated before decisions to abandon them have been hastily taken solely because of their previous ideological associations. For example, at some level, the charismatic appeal of the mass campaign approach to raising literacy levels based on the information-extension approach will almost certainly be missed as adults are shunted off to school-like forms of adult education. As Flora and Flora (1977) observed "this institutionalization but not routinization of charisma [embodied in the Mass Campaign approach] is crucial to the understanding of the Chinese approach to development." Nevertheless, some of the earlier educational innovations may be retained in form, even if their original identify is masked by changing their names.

166. In fact, as one can see from historical recapitulations of the trends in the provision of worker-peasant education, during the periods of post independence (1949-58), the Great Leap Forward (1958-60), the Post-Great Leap Forward (1960-66), and the Cultural Revolution (1966-76), philosophical swings between ideological (political indoctrination) and technical (training) education were mainly reflected in the name changes and the altered content emphasis of institutional forms which remained basically unchanged.

167. Many problems and questions abound when one gazes into China's adult education and development future. As Shirk (1979) has noted, "It is ironic that today, when elements of the Chinese model have become incorporated in development criteria and the policies of some Third World countries, the Chinese themselves seem to be abandoning the model." In a way, Chinese education theory and practice, like those of Western countries, are concentrating on a "back to the basics movement" while the Third World is left with their respective hand-me-downs: the over-implementation of political content, open classrooms, and new math. There is a critical need for the Chinese to scrutinize their past efforts closely

in order to avoid overlooking the good aspects of the adult educational innovations of earlier periods just as there is a need for Western educators to analyze the results of past innovative educational strategies before the wholesale abandonment of them. Especially in China, it is difficult to access empirical evidence on just how effective and efficient such innovations were.

168. Furthermore, there is a general need to establish the comparative cost effectiveness of various adult education efforts, e.g., workers' universities in comparison to regular technical secondary schools or university training, and to balance such economic and financial analyses with assessments of social cost accounting. In addition, existing inequities, such as rates of illiteracy in minority areas /15, unbalanced economic development throughout the country in general, the shortage of teaching materials, and the low quality of educational staff whose knowledge and skills are either incomplete or obsolete, are matters for serious thought and action. In addition, there may indeed be limits to self-reliance from a sheer environmental deprivation point of view. As Unger (1980) has observed in his analysis of the failures of educational reform in China: "The irony was that the best off villages also tended to be the ones already possessing government financed schools. The new programs persuaded the middle range of villages to foot their own school programs and left the

---

/15 The issue in minority education has always been one of promoting cultural identity versus social mobility. During the Cultural Revolution, special programs and institutions for minority peoples were either scaled down or closed in an effort to integrate minority peoples into regular educational programs to promote egalitarianism. As reported in an interview with the Director of the Central Institute for National Minorities, the cultural identity approach was negatively referred to as "Big Han Chauvism." During the Cultural Revolution customs were banned, ethnic clothing prohibited, and books in minority language banned. Today it is currently the view that the Gang of Four mixed the problems of minorities with the issue of class struggle. As stated by an adult education official in Sichuan, they were "revolutionary in appearance but counter-revolutionary in reality, even some of the minorities were deceived." During the period of "restoration" (1976-81) it is felt that the government has done much to make up for the deeds of the 1950s toward National minorities. Examples given of recent actions are: the restoration of bilingual instruction and boarding schools; efforts to eradicate illiteracy in local languages; and a new directive from the Committee on National Languages to restore printing and publishing in such media. There is now a National Minorities Press in Sichuan Province, radio broadcasts in minority languages, and a policy in the Province to release minority peoples from work for one month to resume literacy classes with pay. Books are also distributed at a lower cost through the Government stores to national minorities. The two neighboring autonomous regions also have their own song and dance troops which are revitalizing traditional media and cultures.

poorest villages unwilling to participate." This analysis may apply to adult education as well.

169. The emerging problem of youth unemployment and alienation pose a major challenge to the role of adult education in value formation/16 and production-employment linked training for China over the next decade. As the Kerr Commission (1978) on Education and Work found

> many youths are still 'dumped' into rural areas to avoid unemployment in the cities; are assigned outside their area of preference; and are stuck for life in places they would rather not be. On the other hand, there are places for everybody - no unemployment, no dropouts. It seems strange, however, that a society that seems to do so exceedingly well with children should do so much less well for its youths.

Despite the re-emergence of youth palaces and special youth oriented sparetime schools run by municipal and district authorities, the real question is whether such efforts will be "too little, too late" and thus fail to quell the rising disaffection among youth.

170. Though a review (such as this one) of worker-peasant education in China tends to leave the reader with a feeling of "qualified optimism" about the future of adult education there, many questions remain unanswered. Will formalizing adult education reduce its ability to respond to changing local/individual needs? Or rather will equivalency and certification efforts serve to legitimize adult education and put it on a par with more traditionally accepted forms of schooling? Does the current system of Chinese adult education lead to the development of critical thinking skills or does it merely endeavor to create a disciplined workforce? How do policies and educational offerings simultaneously accommodate the needs of those in rural and urban settings? Of young and old? Of men and women? What efforts need to be made to provide educational and cultural activities for those who are too old to work? As the rapid pace of technology and mechanization eliminate jobs, will there be a need to totally reeducate workers rather than merely upgrade them. Should career counselling/education be made a standard part of educational curricula? How can relevant textbooks be functionally improved? How can they be produced and distributed on a mass scale? Should more energy be placed on developing a variety of teaching media, e.g., films, filmstrips, transparencies, which can be widely distributed? How can formal universities be mobilized to play a more important role in providing continuing adult education? What can China teach the rest of the world about adult education, or *vice-versa*? And how can such an exchange of information best be implemented?

/16 Daycare, forced mobility, and re-education campaigns and programs have been effective mechanisms for breaking down inter-generational patterns of socialization. But to a large extent much value confusion among the young has resulted as those in control of such mechanisms have been replaced once more.

171. The time is ripe for China to evaluate its rich experience in adult education and to share the lessons gleaned from such evaluations with the rest of the world. Clearly, on both sides, there is much to be learned and gained.

BIBLIOGRAPHY

1. Abe, Runemitra, "Spare-time Education in Communist China," China Quarterly, Vol. 8, 149-159.

2. Adult Education in China, Peasants' Education Division, Bureau of Worker-Peasant Education, Beijing: 1980.

3. Baohua, Yuan. "Staff and Worker Education as an Important Means of Developing Intelligence and Fostering Talent," Xinhua, March 19, 1981.

4. Barendsen, Robert D. "The 1960 Education Reforms," China Quarterly (Oct-Dec, 1960): 55-65.

5. ________________. "The Agricultural Middle School in Communist China," China Quarterly 8 (Oct-Dec, 1961): 106-134. Reprinted in China under Mao, pp. 303-332. Edited by R. MacFarquhan. Cambridge: MIT Press. 303-332.

6. ________________. "Education in China: A Survey," Problems of Communism XIII (July-Aug, 1964): 19-27.

7. ________________. Half-work, Half-study schools in Communist China: Recent Experiments with Self-supporting Educational Institutions. Washington, D.C.: U.S. Government Printing Office, Office of Education Bulletins, 1964.

8. ________________ "Mao's Education Revolution," American Education, (May 1972): 4-10.

9. ________________, The Educational Revolution in China. Washington, D.C.: U.S. Government Printing Office, 1975.

10. ________________. Education in the People's Republic of China - A Selective Annotated Bibliography of Materials Published in the English Language (1971-1976), Washington, D.C.: U.S. Government Printing Office, 1981.

11. Bao, Ta Kong. China Hand. Hong Kong: Kwang Yi Printing Press, Ltd., 1980.

12. Bastid, Marianne. "Economic Necessity and Political Ideas in Educational Reform During the Cultural Revolution" in Power and Ideology in Education. Edited by Jerome Karabel and A.H. Halsey. New York: Oxford University Press, 1977.

13. Benstein, Thomas P. Up to the Mountains and Down to the Villages. New Haven: Yale University Press, 1977.

14. Bettelheim, Charles. Cultural Revolution and Industrial Organization in China - Changes in Management and the Division of Labor. New York: Monthly Review Press, 1974.

15. Boping, Zang. "The Role of Adult Education in Socialist Modernization," Red Flag XVI (August 1980): 33-37.

16. Buck, David D. "Cities and Education in Modern China," Comparative Education XI (March 1975): 73-83.

17. Buck, Pearl S. Tell the People - Talks with James Yen about the Mass Education Movement. New York: John Day Company, 1945.

18. Chen, Theodore Hsi-en. "Collective Learning in Communist China's Universities," Far Eastern Survey XXVI (January 1957): 8-11.

19. ________________. "Education" in China: A Handbook. Edited by Yuan-li Wu. New York: Praeger Publishers, 1973.

20. ________________. The Maoist Educational Revolution. New York: Praeger, 1974.

21. ________________. "Changes in Chinese Education," Current History LXXV (September 1978): 75-82.

22. ________________. "Chinese Education after Mao: More Revolutionary or More Academic?" Teachers College Record LXXIX (February 1978): 365-388.

23. Chiang, Monlin. Chinese Culture and Education. Taibei: World Book Company, 1963.

24. Chien. "Development of Systematic Training in Rural Public Health," Annual Report, International Rural Reconstruction Movement (formerly Mass Education Movement), New York: 1935.

25. The Chinese Mass Education Movement - A Summary. Mass Education Movement. December 31, 1944.

26. "Chinese Youth League Official Comments," Xinhua, March 28, 1980.

27. Chi Tung-wei. Education for the Proletariat in Communist China. Hong Kong: Union Research Institute, 1954.

28. Chou, Wu. Report from Tungting - A People's Commune on Taihu Lake. Peking: Foreign Languages Press, 1975.

29. Chow Tse-tsung. The May Fourth Movement: Intellectual Revolution in Modern China. Stanford: Stanford University Press, 1967.

30. Chu, Godwin C. Radical Change Through Communication in Mao's China. Honolulu: University Press of Hawaii, 1977.

31. Chu, Godwin C., editor. Popular Media in China - Shaping New Cultural Patterns. Honolulu: The University Press of Hawaii, 1978.

32. Chu, Godwin and Francis L.K. Hsu, editors, Moving a Mountain-Cultural Change in China. Honolulu: The University Press of Hawaii, 1977.

33. Chui-sam, Tsang. Schools, Society and Progress in China. New York: Pergamon, 1968.

34. Chung-ta, Yao. "Adult Education in China" personal correspondence to J.R. Kidd, China-ICAE Project, Toronto, Ontario, September 1980.

35. Committee of Concerned Asian Scholars. China! Inside the People's Republic. New York: Bantam, 1972.

36. De Francis, John, Nationalism and Language Reform in China, University Press, 1980.

37. Dore, Ronald. The Diploma Disease. Berkeley, California: University of California Press, 1976.

38. "Education in China and Issues Related to Possible Bank Education Financing," draft mimeo. Washington, D.C. Education Department, World Bank, 1981.

39. Flora, Jan L. and Flora, Cornelia B. "Rural Development in the People's Republic of China: A Theoretical Perspective," Rural Sociology XLII (Winter 1977): 476-490.

40. Fraser, Stewart. Education and Communism in China. London: Pall Mall Press, 1971.

41. ___________. Chinese Education: Records of the First Decade. New York: Wiley, 1965.

42. Fraser, Stewart, editor. Chinese Communist Education: Records of the First Decade. Nashville, Tennessee. Vandervilt University Press, 1965.

43. Fraser, Stewart E., and Hawkins, J. "Chinese Education: Revolution and Development," Phi Delta Kappa LII (April 1972): 496-498.

44. Fraser, Stewart E., and Hsu, Kuang-liang. Chinese Education and Society: A Bibliographic Guide. White Plains, New York: International Arts and Sciences Press, 1972.

45. Galt, Howard S. A History of Chinese Educational Institutions. London: Arthur Probsthain, 1951.

46. Gamberg, Ruth. Red and Expert: Education in the People's Republic of China. New York: Schocken Books, 1977.

47. Gardner, John and Idema, Wilt, "China's Educational Revolution" in Authority, Participation and Cultural Change in China. Edited by Stuart R. Schram. Cambridge, England: Cambridge University Press.

48. Harper, P. Spare-Time Education for Workers in Communist China. Washington, D.C.: United States Office of Education, 1964.

49. Hawkins, John N. "Mao Tse-tung and Bureaucracy: The May Seventh Cadre Schools," Journal of Continuing Education and Training I (May 1972): 259-66.

50. __________. "Reschooling Society Chinese Style: Alternative Forms of Nonformal Education," Educational Studies IV (1973).

51. __________. Mao Tse-tung and Education: His Thoughts and Teachings. Hamden, Conneticut: Shoe String Press, 1974.

52. __________. "Rural Education and Technique Transformation in the People's Republic of China," Technological Forecasting and Social Change XI (1978): 315-333.

53. __________. "Educational Change in China: The Post Gang of Four Era."

54. __________. "China: This Society is Communications," Intermedia VIII (March 1980): 10-23.

55. __________. Educational Theory in the People's Republic of China: The Report of Ch'ien Chung-jui. Honolulu: University of Hawaii Press, 1971.

56. __________. "The Education of Minority peoples in the Peoples Republic of China," Comparative Education Review, Vol. 22 No. 2 1978.

57. Hayford, Charles W. "Rural Reconstruction in China: Y. C. James Yen and the Mass Education Movement" 1975, pp. 333. Unpublished thesis, University Microfilm, Ann Arbor, Michigan.

58. Herschede, Fred. "Higher Education and the Expansion of Technically Qualified Industrial Workers During China's Modernization, 1976-1985," Bulletin of Concerned Asian Scholars XI (July-September 1979): 64-71.

59. Hinton, William. Hundred Day War: The Cultural Revolution at Tsinghua University. New York: Monthly Review Press, 1972.

60. Holden, John, et al. "China Today," Lifelong Learning: The Adult Years II (June 1979): 4-9.

61. Howard, Roger. Contemporary Chinese Theatre. Singapore: Hineman Educational Books, Ltd., 1978.

62. Howkins, John. "The Media in China," Educational Broadcasting International Vol. 13 (June 1980): 58-61.

63. __________. "The Society is Communications," Inter Media, Vol. 8 No. 2 (March 1980): 10-18.

64. Hsin Hsueh-wen. "A New Type of College," China Reconstructs XXIV (May 1975): 6-10.

65. Hultin, Mats. Education in China, Washington, D.C.: Education Department, World Bank, 1981.

66. Hu, C. T. "Communist Education: Theory and Practice," China Quarterly X (Apr-June): 84-97. (Reprinted in China under Mao, edited by R. MacFarquhar. Cambridge, Massachusetts: : MIT Press, 241-254.).

67. Hu, C.T., editor. Chinese Education under Communism. New York: Columbia University Teachers College, 1974.

68. Kerr, Clark, editor. Observation on the Relations Between Education and Work in the People's Republic of China - Report of a Study Group, Berkeley, California: Carnegie Council on Policy Studies in Higher Education, 1978.

69. Kobayashi, Fumio. Education in Building Chinese Socialism: Theory and Reality in the Transitional Period. Tokyo: Institute of Developing Economies, 1976.

70. Kobayashi, Victor and King, Tung-rak. "Education in the People's Republic of China: An Update," mimeo. Ann Arbor, Michigan: School of Education, University of Michigan.

71. Kwong, Julia. "The Educational Experiment of the Great Leap Forward, 1958-1959: Its Inherent Contradictions," Comparative Education Review XXIII (October 1979).

72. Lin, Paul T.K. "Development Guided by Values: Comments on China's Road and its Implication," International Development Review. XVII (1975): 2-7.

73. Lin, Vincent Tsing Ching. "Adult Education in People's Republic of China, 1950-58." Unpublished Doctoral Dissertation, University of Berkeley, California: University of California, Unpublished doctoral dissertation, 1963.

74. Liu Yu-sheng. "The Nanniwan May 7 Cadre School," China Reconstructs XXIII (July 1974): 5-9.

75. Lofstedt, Jan-Inguar. Chinese Educational Policy. Stockholm: Almquist and Wiksell, 1980.

76. Lucas, Christopher J. "Adult Education in the People's Republic of China," Adult Education XXVI (1976): 143-156.

77. Mao Zedong. "Talks at the Yenan Forum on Literature and Art" in Selected Works of Mao Tse-Tung, Vol. III. Beijing: Foreign Language Press, 1967. Beijing.

78. McCormick, Robert. "Central Broadcasting and Television University," The China Quarterly, March 1980.

79. ______________. "China's Central Broadcasting and Television University." mimeo comments and recommendations. Open University, March 1981.

80. Mitgang, Herbert. "View of Mao's World in a Book on his Wife," New York Times, March 6, 1977.

81. Munro, Donald J. "Dissent in Communist China: The Current Anti-intellectual Campaign in Perspective," Current Scene IV (June): 1-19.

82. ______________. "Maxims and Realities in China's Education and Policy: The Half-work, Half-study Model," Asian Survey VII (April): 254-272.

83. ______________. "Egalitarian Ideal and Educational Fact in Communist China" in China: Management of a Revolutionary Society, pp. 256-304. Edited by John M. H. Lindback. Seattle: University of Washington Press.

84. Oho Yee To. "Industrial Education in China Today," Education Digest (May 1974): 13-15.

85. Orleans, Leo A. Professional Manpower and Education in Communist China. Washington, D.C.: Government Printing Office, 1961.

86. ________. "Chinese Statistics: The Impossible Dream," The American Statistician (May 1974): 47-52.

87. Parish, William L., and Whyte, Martin K. Village and Family in Contemporary China. Chicago: University of Chicago Press, 1978.

88. Pepper, Suzanne. "Education and Political Development in Communist China." Studies in Comparative Communism III (July-October 1970): 132-57.

89. ______________. "Education After Mao," China Quarterly II, 1980.

90. ______________. "Education and Revolution: The 'Chinese Model' Revisited," Asian Survey XVIII (September 1978): 847-90.

91. Price, R.F. Education in Communist China. New York: Praeger, 1970.

92. ________________. "Labor and Education in Russia and China," Comparative Education X (March 1974): 13-23.

93. ________________. " 'Community and School' , and Education in the People's Republic of China," Comparative Education XII (June 1976): 163-72.

94. Printing, Peggy, and Steinls, Paul. Commune Life in Rural China. Singapore: Times Books International, 1977.

95. Rawski, Evelyn Sakakida. Education and Popular Literacy in Ch'ing China. Ann Arbor, Michigan: University of Michigan Press, 1979.

96. Rogers, E.M. "Barefoot Doctors," in George I. Lythscott et. al. (editors), Report of the Rural Health Systems Delegation to the People's Republic of China. 1978, Washington, D.C.: National Academy of Science.

97. ______________. "Communication and Development in the People's Republic of China." Educational Broadcasting International 13 No. 2 (June 1980): 51-58.

98. Rogers, E.M. and Chen, Pi-chao. "Diffusion of Health and Birth Planning Innovations in the People's Republic of China" in George I. Lythscott et. al. (editors), Report of the Rural Health Systems Delegation to the People's Republic of China, pp. 1-40, 1978, Washington, D.C.: National Academy of Science.

99. Rubrucker, Lee I. "Sparetime Higher Education in the Peoples' Republic of China," Montana State University, doctoral dissertation, 1970.

100. Schram, Stuart. Mao Tse-Tung London: Penguin Books, 1966.

101. Schramm, Wilbur, Chu, Godwin C., and Frederick, T.C. Yu. "China's Experience with Development Communication: How Transferrable is It?" East Lansing, Michigan: Conference on Nonformal Education for the Poor, October 1976.

102. Selden, Mark. The Yenan Way in Revolutionary China. Cambridge, Massachusetts: Harvard University Press, 1971.

103. Seybolt, Peter J., Chinese Education IX, Special Issue on Adult Education. White Plains, New York: M.E. Sharpe Publishers, 1976.

104. ______________. "The Yenan Revolution in Mass Education," China Quarterly XLVIII (October-December 1971): 641-69.

105. ______________. Revolutionary Education in China. White Plains, New York: International Arts and Sciences Press, 1972.

106. ______________. "China's Revolution in Education: The Struggle Between Two Lines," Journal of Canadian and International Education, I (1977): 29-41.

107. Shue, Vivienne. "China: On the Wire." Intermedia, Vol. 8, No. 2 (March 1980): 18-22.

108. Shirk, Susan. "The 1963 Temporary Work Regulations for Full-Time Middle and Primary Schools: Commentary and Translation," China Quarterly LV (July-September 1973): 511-46.

109. __________. "Work Experience in Chinese Education," Comparative Education XIV (March 1978): 5-18.

110. __________. "Educational Reform and Political Backlash: Recent Changes in Chinese Educational Policy," Comparative Education Review XXIII (June 1979): 183-217.

111. Singer, Martin. "Educated Youth and the Cultural Revolution in China," Papers in Chinese Studies X. Ann Arbor, Michigan: University of Michigan Center for Chinese Studies.

112. Sizer, N.F. "John Dewey's Ideas in China, 1919 to 1921," Comparative Education Review X (October 1966): 390-403.

113. "Spare-time College for Beijing's Staff and Workers," Beijing Review XI, March 16, 1981.

114. Tao Hsing-Chih, Translated Papers in Chinese Education, Vol. VII, No. 4, Winter 1974-75.

115. Teiwes, Frederick C. "Before and After the Cultural Revolution," China Quarterly LVIII (April 1974): 332-48.

116. Unger, Jonathan. "Bending the School Ladder: The Failure of Chinese Educational Reform in the 1960s," Comparative Education Review X (June 1980): 221-237.

117. Walls, Jan W. "Popular Media and Social Change: Satire and Modernization in China Today," mimeo. Victoria, British Columbia: Center for Pacific and Oriental Studies, University of Victoria, June 1980.

118. Wang, Hsueh-wen. Chinese Communist Education: The Yenan Period. Taipei: Institute of International Relations, 1975.

119. Wang, James C.F. "The May Seventh Cadre School for Eastern Peking," China Quarterly LXIII (September 1975): 522-27.

120. Wang Wen-yu. "Farm to College and Back to Farm," China Reconstructs XXIV (May 1975): 11-13.

121. Whyte, Martin K. "Education Reform: China in the 1970s and Russia in the 1920s," Comparative Education Review XVIII (February 1974): 112-28.

122. Wong, John. Appropriate Technology and Development - A Review of the Chinese Experience, Occasional Paper No. 3. Singapore: University of Singapore Economic Research Center, 1980.

123. Yao, Zhongda "Adult Education in the People's Republic of China," personal correspondence to J.R. Kidd, China-ICAE Project, Toronto, Ontario, 1980.

124. ____________________ " Introductory Comments on Adult Education in the People's Republic of China", Beijing Symposium on Adult Education, March 1981, Beijing.

125. Yen, James, The Ting Hsien Experiment in 1934. New York: International Institute of Rural Reconstruction, 1934 (reissued 1975).

126. Zachariah, Mathew, "'Mass liners' versus 'Capitalist Roaders' in China's Education Ring: Round Four to 'Capitalist Roaders?'" Comparative Education Review XXIII (February 1979): 101-114.

127. Zhenhua, Lu. "China Enters the Television Age," China Reconstructs XXX (March 1981): 12-17.

Peoples Republic of China

Places Visited and Persons Met

Institution	Key Person(s)
Bureau of Worker and Peasant Education, Ministry of Education	Mr. Yao Zhong-da Deputy Director Bureau of Worker and Peasant Education Mr. Xia Kuai-Sub Unesco National Commission Mr. Wang Yian-Wei Division of Peasant Education Mr. Wang Jian-Tiang Central Institute for Educational Research Mr. Guan Shixiong Director Beijing Bureau of Worker and Peasant Education (and Beijing T.V. University)
Central Institute of National Minorities	Mr. Song Shu-hua Vice President
Beijing General Internal Combustion Engine Factory Spare Time College	Mr. Sha Ji Principal Spare Time College Mr. Chang Nien Lin Vice President of the factory
Beijing Broadcasting and T.V. University	Mr. Guan Shixiong President
Beijing Second Cotton Mill	
Evergreen Peoples Communce Haidian, Beijing	
Symposium (Beijing)	Mr. Sung-Juie Len Director of Education Beijing Municipal Labor Union Mr. Juye Shu Nan Vice President Beijing Textile Plant Sparetime Workers College

	Mr. Wu Tong Wai Beijing Municipal Education Bureau
	Mr. Jie Wei Zheng Vice President Beijing T.V. University
	Mr. Ma Shu Nan Provost Medical Training College Beijing
	Mr. Ren Zun Lian Haidnan District Office for Worker and Peasant Education

Sichuan Province

Sichuan Provincial Department of Education	Mr. Wang Zeng Xian Deputy Minister Provincial Department of Education
Chengdu Rolling Stock Plant Sichuan	Mr. Lui Shao-Hung Plant Vice Director
	Mr. Liu Kokyu Head Peasant Education Division Chengdu
	Mr. Long Gui Yun Pedagogical Research Section for Worker and Peasant Education Chengdu
Xiang Fu Peoples Commune Jing Tang County Sichuan	Mr. Cheng Jia Bin Director Committee for Worker and Peasant Education
	Mr. Diao Gua Jung Director Bureau for Worker and Education
	Mr. Ma Hai Mujia Director Sichuan Provincial Office for Minority Peoples
Chengdu Maternity and Child Hygiene Center, Sichuan	
Dujiangyou Irrigation Works Sichuan	

Shanghai

Shanghai Division of Worker and Peasant Education	Mr. Heng Wei Director Bureau of Education Shanghai
	Mrs. Li Li Director Division of Worker and Peasant Education
	Mr. Wang Ling Deputy Director
Hongkou District Spare Time University, Shanghai	Mr. Fang Jing President
Shanghai Association of Science and Technology	Mr. Yu Chi Jing Director Foreign and Scholarly Relations
	Mr. Zhung Yu Ying Deputy Director Workers Education Department
Shanghai Youth Palace	Mr. Wong Director
Shanghai Municipal Spare Time University	Mr. Lu Wen Tsai Vice President
Shanghai Municipal Library Shanghai Natural Science Museum	Mr. Che Director
Shanghai Workers Palace	Mr. Zhu Chen Zhao Director
Shanyang Peoples Commune Jin Sha County Shanghai Region	Mr. Zhang Wao Hui Commune Director
	Mr. Whang Pin Head of Education
	Mr. Pan Chu Xiong Head of Technical Education
Jin An District No. 2 Workers Spare Time Middle School Shanghai	Mr. Gung Yu Jiax Director
Shanghai Childrens Palace	

Hunan Province

Provincial Bureau of Education Hunan	Mr. Xu Zen Ming President Mr. Sun Yen Vice President Mr. Sha Xing Zi Chief Department of Worker and Peasant Education
Bureau of Worker and Peasant Education Taojing County Hunan	Mr. Sun Tao We Director County Bureau of Education Mr. Xe Bai Jun Director County Office for Worker and Peasant Education
Xiao Shan Wan Brigade School Gaogiao Peoples Commune (combines pre school, primary school and spare time Agro-technical training)	
Zhujinbu Peoples Commune Agro-technical Spare Time School	Mr. Wang Ti Fang Principal
Taojing County Symposium	Range of participants from Commune Directors to Agro-technical school students and County and provincial Bureau of Worker and Peasant Education staff.
Hunan Provincial Level Spare Time Education Committee	Mr. Shin Xin Ying Department of Popularization of Science and Technology Mrs. Tang Xi Ying Mrs. Xia Xing Yuan Provincial Federation of Women Mr. Zhang Lichu Provincial Economic Commission Mr. Lui Zhou and Mr. Yang Zu Provincial Agricultural Bureau Ms. Ding Luang Guang Provincial Communist Youth League

	Mr. Peng Xiang Ling Hunan Daily News
	Mr. Chen Zhen Hunan Radio Station
	Mr. Chang Yong Provincial Trade Union
	Messrs. Zhang Zhaoming and Zhang Xun Zun Provincial Office of Worker and Peasant Education
	(Representatives from finance and trade; Labor Bureau; Construction Committee; Defense and Industry were absent from the Committee meeting)
Hunan Power Machiner Plant	
Majitang Hydraulic Electric Power Station Construction Site Training Taojing County Hunan	
<u>Guandong Province</u>	
Guandong Provincial Education Bureau	Ms. Yang Hang Deputy Director Provincial Department of Education
	Mr. Zhong Bo Yuen Director Provincial Division of Worker-Peasant Education
Guanzchou Heavy Machine Plant	Mr. Han Jing Gua Plant Vice Manager
Guanzchou Municipal Spare Time College	Mr. He Rui Vice President
Conghua County Bureau of Education	Mr. Jian Ye-Ying Deputy Director Bureau of Education
	Mr. Wang Rang Du Chief Section on Worker-Peasant Education
Shawei Production Brigade Longgongtan Peoples Commune Taojing County, Hunan	

Yunxing Production Brigade
Wenquan Peoples Commune
Corghua County
Guangdong Province

Mr. Liong
Production Brigade Head

Ms. Cheng
Deputy Head
Production Brigade

Mr. Li
Director
Brigade, Spare Time Education

Liangming Production Brigade
Liangkou Peoples Commune
Conghue County
Guandong Province

Mr. Ye Gen Pae
Production Brigade Head

Spare Time School
Foshan Branch Bank of Guandong
Province, Chinese Peoples Bank

Guandong Radio and T.V. University
Foshan Branch
Guandong Province

Foshan Wei Man Silk-Textile Factory
Guandong Province

BRIEFS FROM FIELD VISITS

Prepared by Host Chinese Institutions

1. Worker Education

(a) An Introductory Talk on the Education of Staff and Workers in Chengdu Rolling Stock Plant by Liu Shao-hung, vice-director of the plant.

(b) A Brief Introduction to the Educational Work in the Guangzhou (Canton) Heavy Machinery Plant.

(c) Brief Introduction of the Hunan Power Machinery Plant.

(d) Brief Introduction of the Hunan Rubber Plant.

(e) General Condition of the Staff and Workers Education in Beijing General Internal Combustion Engine Plant.

(f) Guangdong Province Foshan - A brief introduction of workers' education condition of Foshan "Wei Man" Silk Textile Factory in March 1981.

(g) General Condition of the Staff and Workers Education Peking Second Cotton Mill.

2. Peasant Education

(a) A Brief Introduction of the Peasants' Education in Conghua County of Guangdong Province in March 1981.

(b) Brief Introduction of the Education of Shawei Brigade of Longgongtan People's Commune in Taojiang County.

(c) Brief Introduction of the Agricultural Spare-time School in Luciduo Commune Taojiang County.

(d) Brief Introduction About the Education in Xiao Shan Wan Production Brigade of Gaoqiao People's Commune in Taojiang County.

(e) Brief Introduction of the Spare-time Agricultural School run by Zhujinba People's Commune in Taojiang County.

(f) Brief Introduction of the Education of Zhongjiaduan Brigade of Longgongtan People's Commune in Taojiang County.

(g) A Brief of Spare-time Education in Shanyang People's Commune

(h) A Brief Introduction of the Education of Xiang Fu People's Commune Jintang County, Sechuan.

(i) Introductory Remarks About the Agrotechnical School Attached to the Evergreen Agricultural Commune, Haidian, Beijing.

3. Provincial/County/Municipal Overviews of Worker-Peasant Education

(a) A Brief Introduction of Adult Education of Taojiang County in Hunan Province - April, 1981

(b) A Brief Introduction of the Peasant Education in Jintang County, Sechuan.

(c) A Brief Introduction to Adult Education in the City of Chengdu by Tun Xi-gen, the deputy director of Chengdu education office.

(d) A Brief Introduction to the Education for the Workers at Yuexiu District of Guangzhou in March,1981.

(e) A Brief Introduction of Adult Education in Sichuan Province.

(f) Worker and Staff Education in Guangzhou.

(g) The Guangzhou Spare-time College.

(h) A Brief Introduction of the Honkow Avocational Institute by Mr. Fang Jing, President.

4. Mass Media

(a) Brief Introductions to Beijing Broadcasting Television University - 1980.

(b) A Brief Introduction to Guangdong Radio & T.V. University, Foshan Branch - March, 1981.

5. Other Institutions

(a) The Brief Introduction About the Staff and Workers Education - the Foshan Branch Bank of Guangdon Province of the Chinese People's Bank in March, 1981.

(b) Briefing of the Spare-time Education on the Construction-site of Majitang Hydraulic Electric Power Station in Taojiang County.

Appendix C

Organization Chart

Bureau of Worker-Peasant Education

Ministry of Education*

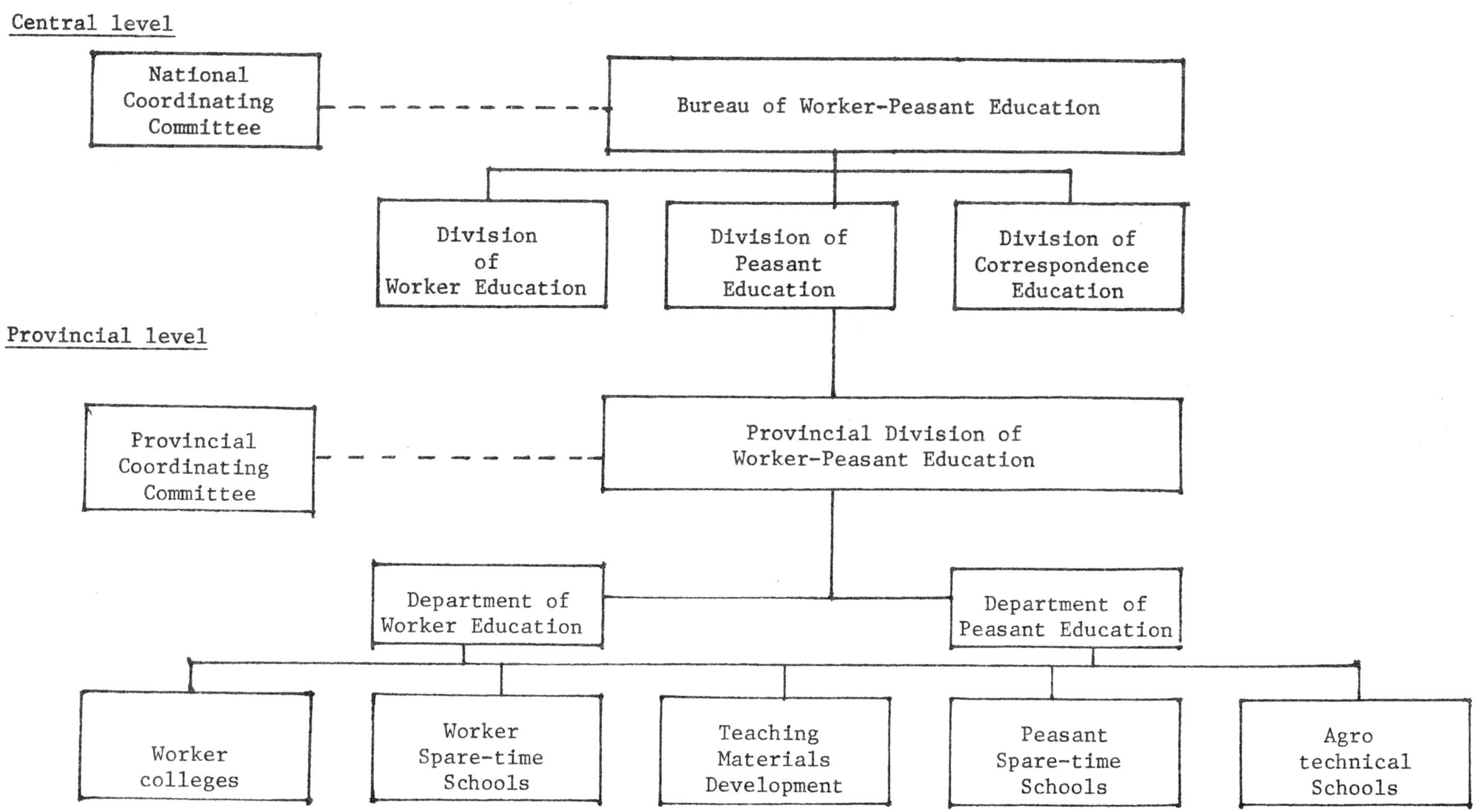

* For organization of Worker-Peasant education at country level and below see Appendices D and E.

Structure Chart of Adult Education in Tao Jiang County

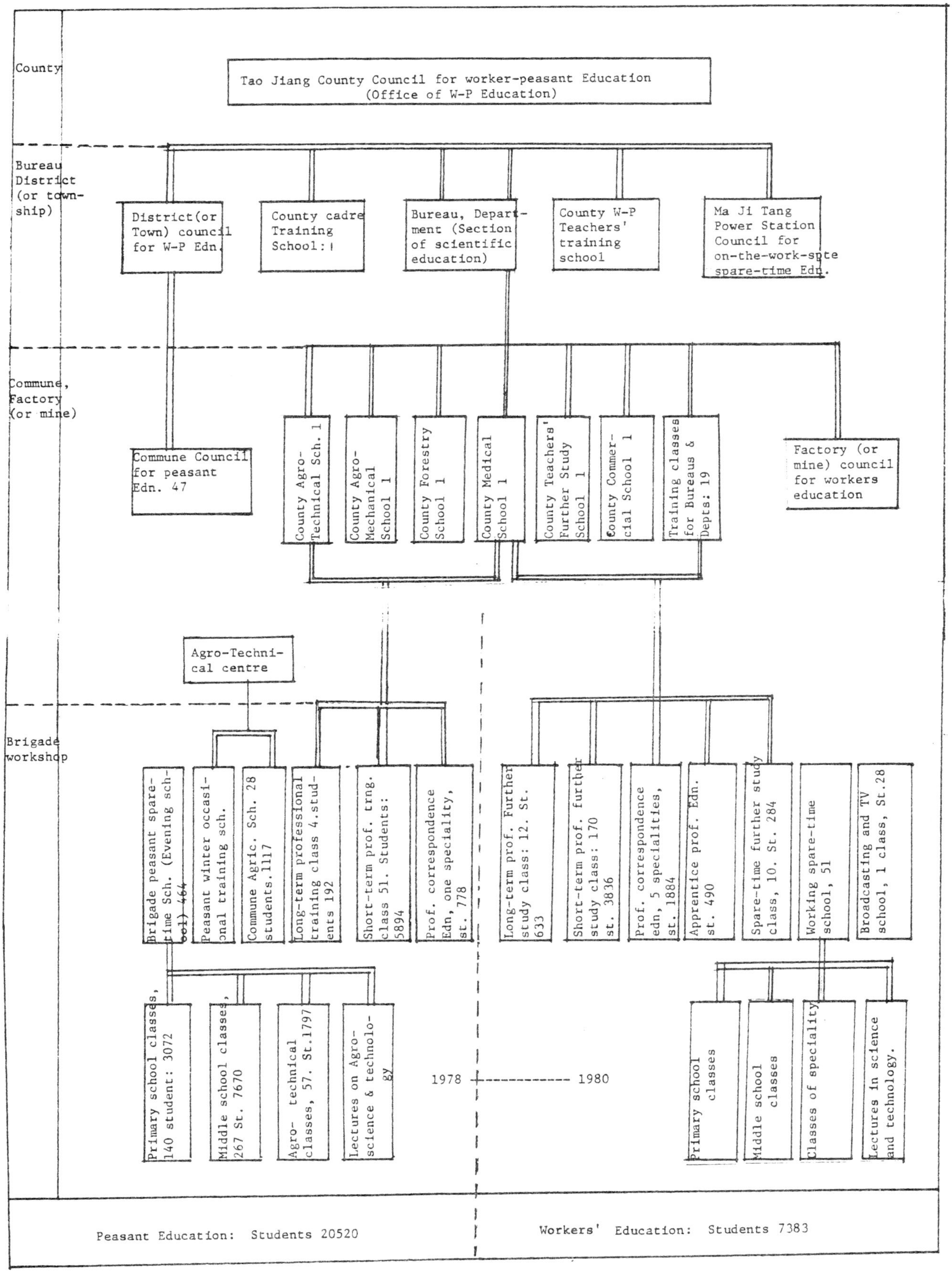

Appendix E

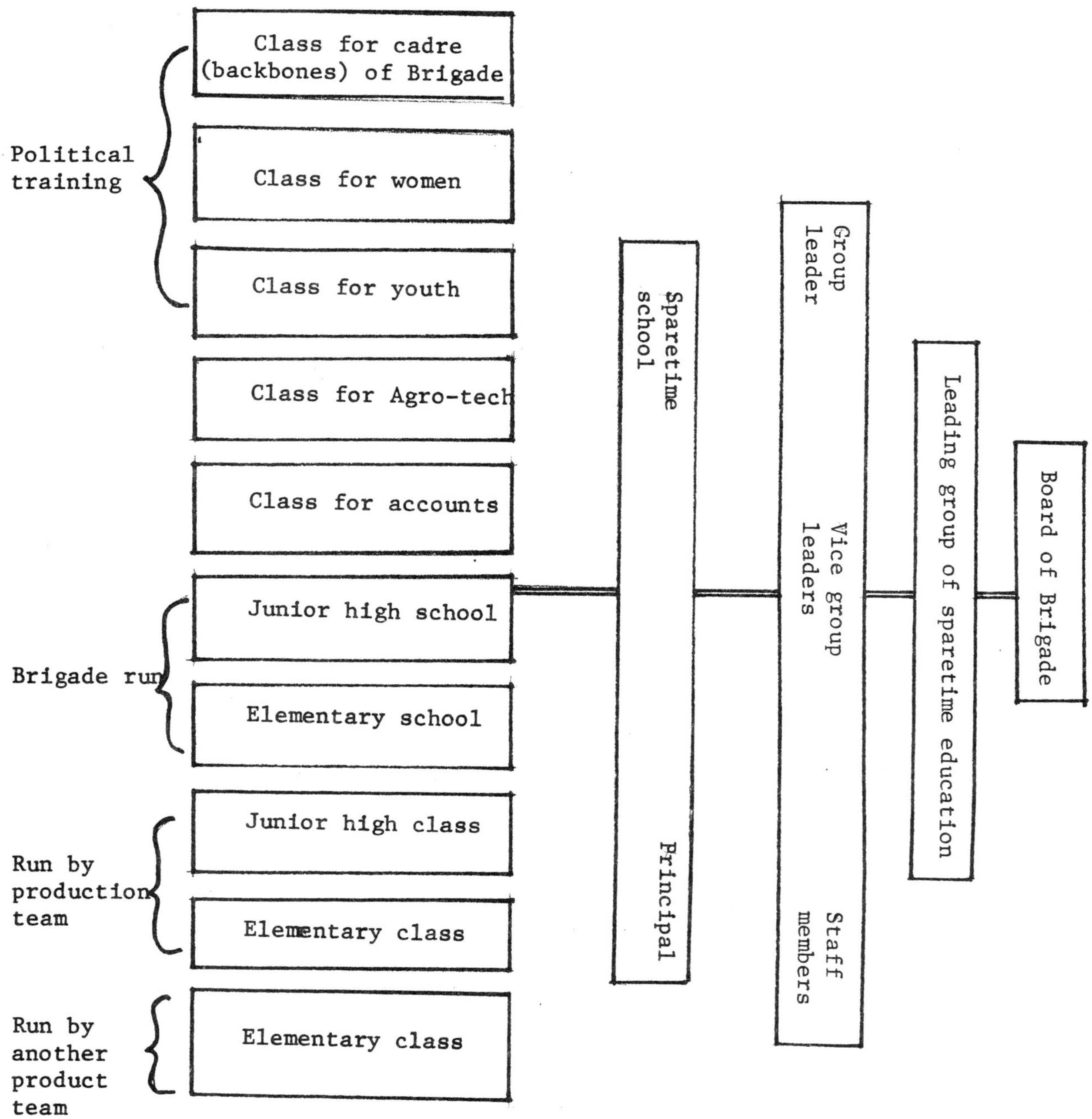

Organization of Yunxing Production Brigade Sparetime Education

Enrollments and Staffing of Select Enterprise Worker Education Programs*

(Enterprise) Factory	No. employees	Enrollment	Staff: Permanent	Staff: Invited	Cost: Capital Yuan	Cost: Operating Yuan
Beijing Internal combustion engine factory	10,200	3,600	57	100	300,000	280,000
Beijing Textile Plant	n.a.	n.a.	50	100	n.a.	n.a.
Chengdu Rolling Stock Plant	4,500	4,380	39	83	36,000	200,000
Hunan Power Machinery Plant	2,144	906	n.a.	n.a.	n.a.	n.a.
Hunan Rubber Plant	n.a.	1,145	n.a.	n.a.	T.V.University 700/yuan/yr Worker University 3000/yuan/yr Spare-time 2,400 yuan/year	
Guanzchou Heavy Machine Plant	6,300	731	29	35	n.a.	n.a.
Foshan "Wai Man" Silk Textile Plant	1,500	1,420	3	32	n.a.	n.a.
Peking Second Cotton Mill	7,600	2,259	40	n.a.	n.a.	n.a.

Notes: * Recurrent costs 2% of 25% of annual workers wages allocated to Union Activities plus variable amount from factory profits.

Operating costs include books and salary of instructor and workers being paid

Admission - recommendation of unit plus exam

Entitlement - each worker right to 6 hrs. education per week

Fees - individual fees are paid by workers for those courses not related to enterprise production.

n.a. - not available

ADULT EDUCATION MATERIALS

TAOJIANG COUNTY - HUNAN PROVINCE

NUMBER	TITLE
001	Illiteracy Eradication Check Cards
002	Illiteracy Eradication Check Cards
003	Empirical Data
004	Local and County Empirical Data
005	Provincial, Local and County Empirical Data
006	Provincial, Local and County Empirical Data
007	Provincial, Local and County Empirical Data
008	Results of Examinations in Sparetime Middle and Elementary Schools
009	Sparetime Middle and Elementary Examination Registration Cards
010	Middle and Elementary Inspection Results
011	Sparetime Middle and Elementary Examination and Inspection Results
012	Sparetime Middle and Elementary Examination and Inspection Results
013	Model Experiences
014	Model Surveys
015	Summary of Illiteracy Eradication Work
016	Summary of Work Over the Years
017	Summary Data
018	Summary Data
019	Summary Report
020	Summary of Illiteracy Eradication Work in the Fifties
021	Power Plant Site Sparetime Education Data
022	Work Bulletin
023	Daily Work Log
024	Regulations for Full-time Cadres in Worker-Peasant Education
025	Model Speeches by Model Workers
026	Model Speeches by Model Workers

027 18 Annexes to the Report to the Central Committee

028 Leadership Talks

029 County Committee, Propaganda Department, Culture and Education Bureau and Sparetime Education Group Documents

030 Documents from the National Education Work Conference

031 Drafts Relating to Data

032 Empirical Data

033 Some Statistics on County Worker-Peasant Education Classes and Partial Culture-Education Classes

034 County, Regional and Commune Communications Report

035 Speeches and Some Individual Experiences Concerning County Committee, Culture and Education Bureau and Worker-Peasant Education Classes

036 Report on Central Committee Documents, Leadership Talks and Education

037 Circulars from All Party Organization Levels Relating to Sparetime Education Work

038 Work Summaries and Related Statistics

039 Various Worker-Peasant School Reports for Future Reference

040 Individual Empirical Data

041 Labor Education Data

042 Preschool Education Data

043 Minutes of the Sparetime Education Work Conference

044 Summary of Sparetime Education Work

045 Partial Unit Individual Draft Speeches

046 Local and County Senior Representative Meeting Materials

047 Regional Worker-Peasant Education Summaries and Plans

048 Model Data

049 Roll of Teenage Illiterates and Semi-illiterates

050 Partial Roll of Commune Teenage Illiterates and Semi-illiterates

051 Empirical Data: Regions 1, 2

052 Sparetime Education Work Data: Regions 1, 2, 3, 5

053 Summary of Sparetime Education Work Data: Regions 2, 4, 6, 7, 8

054 Sparetime Illiteracy Eradication Education Survey: Regions 1, 2, 3, 4, 5

055 Sparetime Education Work Survey Data: Regions 6, 7, 8, 9, 10

056 Partial Regional, Commune, Brigade and Individual Empirical Data

057 Statistical Tables for the Taogushan Region

058 Statistical Tables and Data for the Taohuajiang Region

059 Some Statistics and Tables for the Xiushan Region

060 Statistical Tables for the Sandangjie Region

061 Empirical Data for the Xiushan and Sandangjie Regions

062 Empirical Data for the Daligang Region

063 Empirical Data for the Wutan Region

064 Compilation of Sparetime Education Work Data for Regions 6, 7, 8

065 Empirical Data for Majitang Region (1)

066 Empirical Data for Majitang Region (2)

067 Empirical Data for the Shanshuyu and Huishangang Regions

068 Roll of Illiterate and Semi-illiterate Teenagers in the Shanshuyu Region

069 Empirical Data for the Songmutang Region

070 Provincial and Local Leadership Talks and Outside Empirical Data

071 Documents Issued by the Education Department, the Education Office, the Local-County Education Department, the County Committee and Other Units

072 Talks by Leading Provincial and Local Comrades and Partial Outside Empirical Data

073 Documents and Materials from the Provincial Peasant Education Conference (March, 1980)

074 Outside Reports and Communications

075 Outside Model Data (1)

076 Outside Model Data (2)

September, 1980

SHAWEI BRIGADE SPARETIME EDUCATION PLAN

1. Guiding Principle

Vigorously promote rural sparetime education, quickly raise the level of cultural and scientific knowledge among rural children, youths and adults, achieve a solid foundation for agricultural modernization.

2. Form of Schooling

In accordance with the concrete conditions in our brigade, three classes will be set up:

The sparetime junior middle class will be set up in the Shawei Elementary School, under the leadership of teacher Xue Shangguang. He will also be responsible for language instruction. The cash crop class will be set up on the brigade's tea plantation under the leadership of comrade Hu Jianjun. The agricultural skills class will be led by comrade Xue Qicai.

3. Length of Schooling

Sparetime junior middle school: graduation after two years.
Cash crop class: graduation after two years.
Agricultural skills class: graduation after one year.

4. Class Content

Sparetime junior middle: language and mathematics (including abacus).
Cash crop: soils, cultivation, harvesting, etc.
Agricultural skills: Soils, paddy rice, wheat and rape cultivation; disease and pest prevention, scientific use of fertilizers, water, etc.

5. Study Principles

More intense study during slack agricultural periods, less study during busy agricultural periods. Suspension of classes during intensely busy periods. Summer classes when possible.

Student enrollment is strictly voluntary. Enrollment is free of charge (includes textbooks, notebooks, lamp oil, ink, etc., all to be borne publicly).

6. Class Time

Sparetime junior middle: no fewer than 40 evenings (80 periods).

Cash crop: at least 25 sessions.

Agricultural skills: Centering on links in the production chain, no fewer than 15 sessions for the entire period.

7. Study Discipline

A. Students must observe study discipline. The established class times must be maintained. No late arrivals, early departures, skipping classes.

B. In class, attention must be paid to the lecture and homework must be conscientiously completed.

C. No disruptive talking during class, no joking.

D. Respect public property; conserve lamp oil.

E. Study together and help one another; ask questions when you do not understand. Relate knowledge to reality to solve problems.

8. Instructional Requirements

A. Each comrade in charge of a class must organize his students, follow the study plan, and complete his instructional task.

B. Each instructor must conscientiously study the teaching materials, conscientiously prepare for class, and conscientiously explain the lesson.

C. Assign homework when required; read and criticize promptly.

D. In lecturing, seek to do your best to increase instructional results. Seek to solve thoroughly any concrete problems.

9. Organizational Structure

A. The brigade will hire a secretary. The instructors will form a sparetime education guidance group to oversee instruction.

B. Each class will appoint a class leader to organize study, propaganda instruction, etc.

10. Develop Comparisons and Assessments

In order to promote study and achieve results, at the end of the term carry out a comparison and assessment to select the outstanding students and most enthusiastic participants, to be given prizes by the brigade.

11. Strive for Recognition and Respect

A. Members of the guidance group must file a report with the brigade and strive to receive recognition on solving concrete problems.

B. Persons responsible for the classes must work at encouraging the students and seeing that their study is considered important.

C. Strive to ensure that the students take their studies seriously and not skip classes.

D. Do good propaganda work among the masses to ensure that they take sparetime education seriously.

E. Strive to see that instructors are respected. Offer advice and suggestions.

THIS WEEK'S TELEVISION PROGRAMS

Monday, April 13

Channel 1 (Central Broadcasting Station)

17:30 Pulse Circuit (33)
18:20 English Lecture (1-10-9)
19:00 Network News
19:30 Hygiene and Health: Birth Control Is a Must (Gansu Broadcasting Station)
19:50 Hunan Opera: The Hundred Flowers (performed by the Hunan Provincial Hunanese Opera Troup)

Channel 9 (Hunan Broadcasting Station)

19:00 Network News
19:30 Weekly Opera: "The Hero's Terrace," a selection from the Hunanese opera The Hundred Flowers.
19:35 Hunan News
19:45 Fine Arts Film: The Three Monks
20:05 Science Film: Flying Beyond the Earth

Tuesday, April 14

Channel 1 (Hunan Broadcasting Station)

17:30 English Lecture (1-10-9)
18:00 Middle School Basic Mathematics Lecture: Algebra (42)
19:00 Network News
19:30 Weekly Opera
19:35 Hunan News
19:45 Science Film: Mechanization of Bulk Foodstuffs Transport
20:05 The Hundred Flower Garden: Chen Ailian and the Snake Dance
20:15 Television Play: Mother Was a Slave (Zhejiang Broadcating Station)

Channel 9 (Central Broadcasting Station)

19:00 Network News
19:30 Cultural Life (31): Peking Hand-painted Spun Silk Wall Paintings
19:45 Television Film: Wind and Sun
20:15 Fiction Film: The Lin Family Store
21:35 Selections from performances by the Shizuko Ken Fuji Secondary School's Music Class during their tour of China

Wednesday, April 15

Channel 1 (Central Broadcasting Station)

17:30 Pulse Circuit (34)
18:20 English Lecture (1 - Review 2 - 1)
19:00 Network News
19:30 Comic Dialogue: Welcome to Peking Withered Trees in Spring
20:00 Television Play: The Demon Chasers (Sichuan)

Channel 9 (Hunan Broadcasting Station)

19:00 Network News
19:30 Weekly Opera
19:35 Hunan News
19:45 Be Healthy: Preventing Rabies
19:55 Peking Opera: The Blood-Spattered Palace (Performed by the Changde Peking Opera Troup)

Thursday, April 16

Channel 1 (Hunan Broadcasting Station)

17:30 English Lecture (1 - Review 2 - 1)
18:00 Middle School Basic Mathematics Lecture: Geometry (22)
19:00 Network News
19:30 Weekly Opera
19:35 Hunan News
19:45 Worldwide Science and Technology: Human Oddities
19:55 Fine Arts Film: Performing Artists
20:15 Korean Stories: A Nurse's Story

Channel 9 (Central Broadcasting STation)

19:00 Network News
19:30 Children's Program: "Five Talks and Four Beauties" The Red Flower Blooms
Lyric Prose: White Forest Springs
20:00 Live broadcast of Chinese-Korean men's and women's friendship basketball competition

Friday, April 17

Channel 1 (Central Broadcasting Station)

17:30 Pulse Circuit (35)
18:20 English Lecture
19:00 Network News
19:30 International News
19:40 Science and Technology: Science and technology news in brief: Part 2
19:50 Northern Opera: Thank You, Spring (Liaoning Broadcasting Station)

Channel 9 (Hunan Broadcasting Station)

19:00 Network News
19:30 Weekly Opera
19:35 Hunan News
19:45 Documentary: Wondrous Sights of Huangshan
20:05 Fiction Film: The Second Handshake

Saturday, April 18

Channel 1, 9 (Central Broadcasting Station)

17:30	English Lecture (1 - Review 2 - 2)
18:00	Middle School Basic Mathematics Lecture: Algebra (43)
19:00	Network News
19:30	All Over China: Mount Lao (Shandong Broadcasting Station)
19:50	A Window on Physical Education (100) (1) Judo (2) Acrobatics
20:00	Fiction Film: Three Missing People
21:25	Concert: Songs and Dances performed by the Air Force Political Headquarters of the Chine People's Liberation Army

Sunday, April 19

Channel 1 (Central Broadcasting Station)

8:30	Children's Program: Bookbag on My Shoulder Little Experiment: water pressure Performance organized by the Ancient Music Group (2)
9:05	Television Series Play: Madame Curie (3)
10:00	Fiction Film: Road Test
14:00	Sunday English: Zhenni and Xingxing
14:50	Chamber Music Concert
19:00	Network News
19:30	Atongmu the Mighty (20)
20:00	All Over the World: Syria Today
20:20	Investigating and Pondering: A Visit to the Kowloon Pass
20:40	Television Play: The Broken Bowl (Tianjin Broadcasting Station)
21:35	The Dance Art of Shang Xiaoyun

Channel 9 (Hunan Broadcasting Station)

19:00	Network News
19:30	Atongmu the Mighty (20)
20:00	Weekly Opera
20:05	Hunan News
20:15	The Red Turban: Little Gold Goose Returns to the Flock (Guang-dong Broadcasting Station)
20:25	Unsung Heroes (15): The Pitch-black Night

Basic Statistics

Yunxing and Liangming Brigades

1981

Demographic Basic Productive Indicis	Yunxing Production Brigade	Liangming Production Brigade
Production Teams	13	12
Families	313	415
Population	1770	2156
Laborers	650	758
Cultivated Land	1900(ha)	133 (ha)
Hill area	300 (ha)	80 (ha)
Total Yield (grains)	1075 (ton)	930627 (Kilo)

Basic Education Statistics	1952				1981			
	Classes		Students		Classes		Students	
	Yunxing	Liangming	Yunxing	Liangming	Yunxing	Liangming	Yunxing	Liangming
Nursury	-	-	-	-	1	2	60	57
Primary	20	3	50	102	10	14	422	481
Sparetime	-	-	-	-	10	4	272	78
Jr. Middle School	-	-	-	-	2	-	70	-
Illiteracy	-	-	243 (92%)	758 (87%)	-	10 (13%)		626 (18%)

XIANG FU PEOPLE'S COMMUNE
BASIC DATA

General Data

Commune population	-	21,393
Area 17,282 mu	-	.81 mu per person

Agriculture station/farm tool/sideline industries - cement, light bulb, wire, wine, silver/3179 biogas units/1 construction team/1 broadcasting station/1 supply station/15 brigades/4556 households/115 production teams of about 100 people each/1 hospital/15 clinics/1 middle high school/16 primary schools/13 criches/1 cultural center.

Literacy Results 1952-1981

915 can write letters; 20 can do math; 741 can write notes; 30 play role of teachers; 896 can read news magazines; 336 can read general documents.

Production Indicators	1977		1980
Production output	19,594,767	Jin	21,313,369
Enterprise	733,241	Yuan	3,506,000
Total agriculture	2,728,096		4,644,184
Oil seed	920,965		1,519,235
Industry/sideline production	340,593		1,106,931
Income	1,705,530		3,040,344
Per capita	84		142
Pigs	20,350		25,981

Material Goods & Savings

Bicycles	2,222
Radios	750
T.V.	21
Sewing Machines	210
Recorders	1
Cameras	1
Address Loud Speaker	1
Watches	2,562
Loud Speaker Wire	3,750
Savings	178,400

Appendix K

EDUCATION
CHINA ENROLLMENT PYRAMID 1979
INCLUDING FORMAL AND NON-FORMAL EDUCATION*

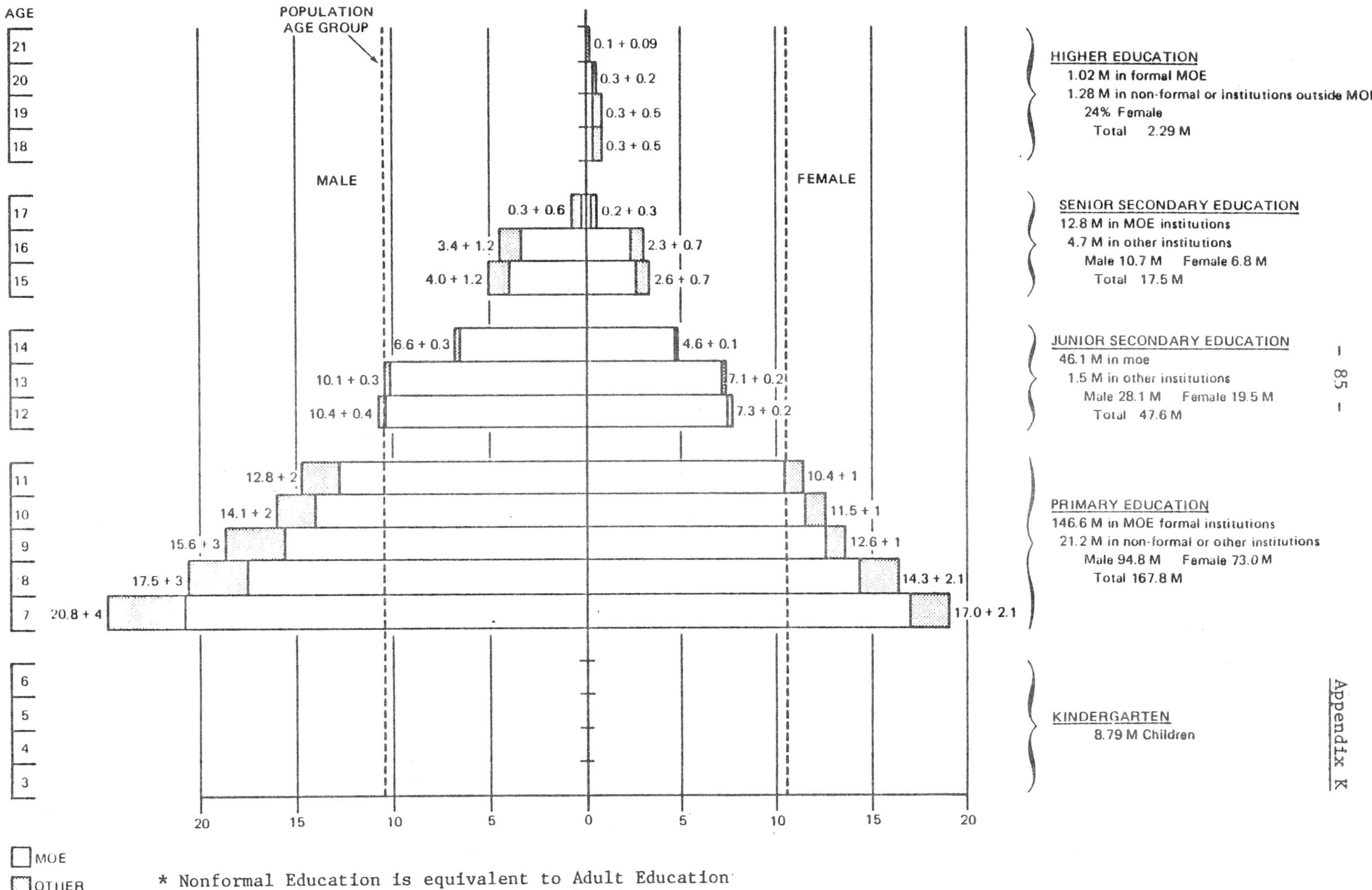

* Nonformal Education is equivalent to Adult Education enrollments as represented by the darkened areas.

World Bank -- 22430

APPENDIX L

EDUCATION IN CHINA

Students, Schools and Teachers in Nonformal Education, 1979

Primary Level

- 21.2 million students, of whom 16.4 million are in literacy courses.

Secondary - Postsecondary Level

- 4.7 million students, of whom 1.5 million are estimated to be in junior secondary education, 0.6 million in general senior secondary education, 2.2 million in technical secondary education and 0.4 million in technical postsecondary education. Full-time students are estimated at 0.6 million, while the rest are spare-time students.

University Level

- 200,000 students are in full-time studies and 660,000 students are in spare-time courses (TV, correspondence, night schools, etc.).

Teachers in Nonformal Education

Full-time	
Primary education	- 0.120 million
Secondary education	- 0.026 million
Higher education	- 0.020 million
Part-time	
Primary education	- 1.000 million
Secondary education	- 0.135 million
Higher education	- 0.033 million

Source: Hultin, 1981

World Bank Publications of Related Interest

Education and Basic Human Needs
Abdun Noor

Conceptualizes basic education and examines its ability to help the poor acquire skills that enable them to meet their basic needs. Groups countries into four major categories and suggests policy choices—based on the unique socioeconomic circumstances and stage of development of countries in each category—that will make basic education universal by the year 2000.

World Bank Staff Working Paper No. 450. April 1981. iv + 64 pages (including 2 annexes).

Stock No. WP-0450. $5.00.

Farmer Education and Farm Efficiency
Dean T. Jamison and Lawrence J. Lau

This book complements earlier studies by reviewing existing literature on the relation between farmer education and farm efficiency. The authors then are able to confirm these earlier findings—which strongly suggest that the more educated farmers are more productive, particularly where new inputs and methods are available—by using new techniques to examine new data sets from Korea, Malaysia, and Thailand. Price data from Thailand are used to test the effect of education on the ability of a farmer to adjust the prices and composition of his output to the prevailing prices.

The Johns Hopkins University Press, April 1982. About 216 pages (including bibliography, appendixes, index).

LC 81-47612. ISBN 0-8018-2575-X, $18.50 hardcover.

Ability in Pre-Schoolers, Earnings, and Home Environment
Roger Grawe

World Bank Staff Working Paper No. 322. April 1979. 92 pages (including appendix, bibliography).

Stock No. WP-0322. $5.00.

Attacking Rural Poverty: How Non-Formal Education Can Help
Philip H. Coombs and Manzoor Ahmed

Educational efforts outside the formal school system that offer potential for rural development and productivity.

The Johns Hopkins University Press, 1974; 3rd paperback printing, 1980. 310 pages (including 3 appendixes, references, index).

LC 73-19350. ISBN 0-8018-1600-9, $25.00 (£11.00) hardcover; ISBN 0-8018-1601-7, $10.95 (£4.25) paperback.

Spanish: La lucha contra la pobreza rural: el aporte de la educación no formal. *Editorial Tecnos,* 1975.

ISBN 84-309-0559-6, 725 pesetas.

Cost-Benefit Analysis in Education: A Case Study of Kenya
Hans Heinrich Thias and Martin Carnoy

Attempts to measure the benefits of various types of education in monetary terms, and to assess the role of earnings in the demand for and supply of educated people in a country.

The Johns Hopkins University Press, 1972. 208 pages (including 5 annexes, bibliography).

LC 72-187064. ISBN 0-8018-1335-2, $6.95 (£4.25) paperback.

A Cost of Siblings: Child Schooling in Urban Colombia
Nancy Birdsall

World Bank Reprint Series: Number 160. Reprinted from Research in Population Economics, *vol. 2 (1980):115-50.*

Stock No. RP-0160. Free of charge.

The Economic Evaluation of Vocational Training Programs
Manuel Zymelman

A methodology for appraising the cost effectiveness of alternative methods of industrial training in developing countries.

The Johns Hopkins University Press, 1976. 134 pages (including chart, 3 appendixes, bibliography).

LC 76-4868. ISBN 0-8018-1855-9, $6.00 (£3.50) paperback.

Spanish: Programas de formación profesional: su evaluación económica. *Editorial Tecnos, 1977.*

ISBN 84-309-0747-5, 415 pesetas.

Education
Wadi D. Haddad, coordinating author

Emphasizes the pervasive role of education in development and draws extensively on the Bank's experience in education for two decades and its close collaborative ties with other international agencies, individuals, and institutions of developing countries.

Sector Policy Paper. April 1980. 143 pages (including 18 annexes, map). English, French, Spanish, Japanese, and Arabic.

Stock Nos. PP-8002-E, PP-8002-F, PP-8002-S, PP-8002-J, PP-8002-A. $5.00.

Educational and Economic Effects of Promotion and Repetition Practices
Wadi D. Haddad

World Bank Staff Working Paper No. 319. March 1979. 52 pages (including 3 annexes, bibliography).

Stock No. WP-0319. $3.00.

Education and Income
Edited by Timothy King; prepared by Mary Jean Bowman; George Psacharopoulos; Marlaine E. Lockheed, Dean T. Jamison, and Lawrence J. Lau; Albert Berry; and Gary S. Fields

World Bank Staff Working Paper No. 402. July 1980. viii + 315 pages (including appendix, bibliography).

Stock No. WP-0402. $5.00.

Education Programs and Projects: Analytical Techniques, Case Studies, and Exercises
Irving A. Sirken

World Bank (EDI), January 1977; revised edition, 1979. ix + 287 pages. (Available from ILS, 1715 Connecticut Avenue, N.W., Washington, D.C. 20009, U.S.A.) $6.00 paperback.

The Effects of Education on Health
Susan Hill Cochrane and others

World Bank Staff Working Paper No. 405. July 1980. 95 pages.

Stock No. WP-0405. $5.00.

The Evaluation of Human Capital in Malawi
Stephen P. Heyneman

World Bank Staff Working Paper No. 420. October 1980. vi + 101 pages (including references, 21 tables, 6 annexes).

Stock No. WP-0420. $5.00.

Higher Education in Developing Countries: A Cost-Benefit Analysis
George Psacharopoulos

World Bank Staff Working Paper No. 440. November 1980. 129 pages (including references, tables).

Stock No. WP-0440. $5.00.

Investment in Indian Education: Uneconomic?
Stephen P. Heyneman

World Bank Staff Working Paper No. 327. May 1979. 56 pages (including bibliography, annex).

Stock No. WP-0327. $3.00.

Primary Schooling and Economic Development: A Review of the Evidence
Christopher Colclough

World Bank Staff Working Paper No. 399. June 1980. 31 pages (including references, 5 tables).

Stock No. WP-0399. $3.00.

Priorities in Education: Preschool; Evidence and Conclusions
M. Smilansky

World Bank Staff Working Paper No. 323. April 1979. ii + 72 pages (including appendix, references).

Stock No. WP-0323. $5.00.

Public Expenditures on Education and Income Distribution in Colombia
Jean-Pierre Jallade

Examines the allocation of educational benefits among various population groups and considers the distributional effects on taxes that pay for public subsidies in general.

The Johns Hopkins University Press, 1974. 90 pages (including 2 annexes, bibliography).

LC 74-4216. ISBN 0-8018-1628-9, $5.00 (£3.00) paperback.

Publishing for Schools: Textbooks and the Less Developed Countries
Peter H. Neumann

World Bank Staff Working Paper No. 398. June 1980. ii + 79 pages (including 2 appendixes).

Stock No. WP-0398. $5.00.

Student Learning in Uganda: Textbook Availability and Other Factors
Stephen P. Heyneman and Dean T. Jamison

World Bank Reprint Series: Number 163. Reprinted from Comparative Education Review, *vol. 24, no. 2 (June 1980):206–20.*

Stock No. RP-0163. Free of charge.

Teacher Training and Student Achievement in Less Developed Countries
Torsten Husen, Lawrence J. Saha, and Richard Noonan

World Bank Staff Working Paper No. 310. December 1978. ii + 133 pages (including annex, bibliography).

Stock No. WP-0310. $5.00.

Why Impoverished Children Do Well in Ugandan Schools
Stephen P. Heyneman

World Bank Reprint Series: Number 111. Reprinted from Comparative Education, *vol. 15, no. 2 (June 1979):175–185.*

Stock No. RP-0111. Free of charge.